Defining Literacy Levels

By Brenda M. Weaver

Weaver, Brenda., 1950-
Defining literacy levels.
p. 257 cm. 22
ISBN 0-87157-849-2
Includes bibliographical references.
SUMMARY: Intended for teachers using the whole language approach for teaching chil-
dren to learn to read and a means of assessment for this process.
1. Whole language. 2. Language arts.
I. Title.
LB1776.W4 1992
372.6

Dedicated to the Skaneateles teachers, administrators, children, and parents who believe in, support, and promote the whole language philosophy.

Contents

Acknowledgments

Whole language is a collaborative process and, therefore, many people are to be thanked for their support in the writing of this book. Thank you to everyone who has had a share in this process.

This book would not have been possible without the dedication and commitment of the Skaneateles teachers. The questions, suggestions, comments, and hard work from these teachers have helped to shape the Skaneateles Language Arts Program, an Exemplary Reading Program (award presented by the International Reading Association, May 1992). These teachers make the program work.

I would also like to thank the Skaneateles principals: Jack Palombella, Marilyn Greer, and Bill Britt for their support and assistance in developing the program. The teachers would not have had the opportunity to embark on this wonderful adventure of whole language without them. They have helped build the foundation of tomorrow's education.

A special thank you to Dr. Walter Sullivan, superintendent, and the Skaneateles Board of Education for their belief in and support of my work and the whole language philosophy. They are the true champions of children and excellence in education.

I would like to express my appreciation to Dr. Diane Sawyer, presently a professor at Middle Tennessee State University, for her suggestions, comments, and program modifications resulting from her evaluation study of our whole language program. A special thank you to Dr. Sawyer for her endless hours of discussion and input into the conceptual development of the literacy levels. The development of these literacy levels is so much richer for her contribution.

Lastly, and most importantly, I would like to thank the Skaneateles students who blossomed into life-long readers and writers. They are an inspiration to us all. This adventure into the education of the 21st century — whole language — is worth all the hard work because the children are our future.

Preface

Some say whole language is only a fad or a phase in American education. Others say it is a paradigm shift into a different American educational system. I say that the proof is in how American teachers practice whole language. Most educators can agree the philosophy and belief systems of whole language are enticing and helpful to children's learning. Research seems to support this perspective of learning. However, the practice of whole language seems to have many different interpretations. Some teachers claim they are teaching whole language because they use big books. Others say that whole language is using literature. Moreover, others say that children in whole language are not taught skills or only write independently by choice.

As a Language Arts Coordinator, accountable to teachers, administrators, and parents, I believe there must be a blending of what was known before as "good teaching" and whole language teaching. This apparent conflict between traditional teachers and whole language teachers presents an either/or solution and I feel the solution is a combination of both: traditional and whole language. For example, most educators are aware of the research which states that phonics is useful in learning to read and write. This research comes out of the traditional approach, but the interpretation is very different in whole language. In whole language, phonics is used to spell words while writing. In reading, phonics is used in the story to pronounce unfamiliar words when the context fails to help children pronounce the word. This results in the blending of both research bases and provides for a stronger foundation in the instruction of the language arts.

The attempt of this book is to assist teachers in moving from traditional practice to whole language practice as interpreted by the author through the Skaneateles Language Arts Program. People will bring to this book their own prior experiences and mindsets about what whole language should or should not be. It is not the intent of this author to describe "the American whole language program" but rather one whole language program which built upon one American school culture. This program integrates the research, both traditional and whole language, into a time tested approach to the language arts. The author is hopeful that this book will provide some assistance to teachers and schools struggling with the practice of whole language in an American setting. Best of luck into the adventure of whole language teaching.   B. M. W.

Introduction

Do you believe in the whole language philosophy? Do you have knowledge of the theory base? Have you tried whole language activities in your classroom? Are you confused about how to put all the pieces of a whole language program together? Are you concerned about how to select what should be taught, when, and to whom? Are you using the monitoring system of a basal reader to keep you on track? If the answer to all of these questions is yes, then this book is intended for you.

This book is intended to assist teachers in understanding whole language, whole language teaching, and the literacy levels in reading and writing for children who are learning to read and write. Through this book, I hope also to provide teachers with a means for the selection of books to use in their whole language program.

In 1987 our school district developed a plan to implement the whole language approach to language arts. Our goals were to develop life-long readers and writers, integrate the language arts, increase the writing experiences of our students, and maintain and/or improve achievement. Our district also employed an outside evaluator, Dr. Diane Sawyer, Director of the Reading Clinic, Syracuse University, to assess and evaluate the implementation process.

At the initial stages of implementation, the shared reading experience or whole class reading instruction was predominately utilized for teaching children to learn to read. Moreover, reading skills were predominately taught within the context of the story. However, during those initial stages teachers began to notice that some students, especially academically below — average students, had to be given more structured, small group instruction. The teachers began to ask me for more specific guidelines in the development of reading in the whole language approach. They asked: Where, when, and how do we introduce specific reading skills like phonics, main idea, contractions, and adjectives? How do we know when they need more practice or when they've learned it? Most of the whole language literature I had read seemed to indicate that reading skills will come naturally or were otherwise vague.

During the initial stages of this implementation, I was fortunate to receive a scholarship, sponsored by the New York State Education Department, to study the whole language approach in New Zealand. As a result of my observations, reading of whole language literature, and my own knowledge and understanding of reading/writing theory and instruction, I began to define a structure of reading/writing development that could help transition teachers from the traditional basal reader approach to a whole language approach. Using the New Zealand Ready to Read program as a base, a framework was developed for teachers in reading/writing development. This framework included behaviors, strategies, skills, and assessment. This book describes this reading/writing framework for teaching children and gives teacher guidelines for implementation.

Utilizing this learning to read/write framework as well as all of the other aspects of the whole language approach, our district evaluation has shown that this whole language program is successful. Our children read and write more than students in the past (supported by double circulation in the school library, local writing test data, language arts portfolios, and survey data), have maintained their academic standing according to their ability (standardized test data), and share a love of reading and writing (teacher and parent observations).

The primary purposes of this book are:

-to describe goals and a framework for classroom experiences in developing literacy using a whole language approach

-to provide guidelines for instruction and assessment in this learning to read/write structure

-to assist teachers in understanding reading/writing development in a whole language approach

-and to provide a means for selecting books at various literacy levels to assist children on the road to literacy

Chapter 1 Defining Whole Language

Whole language is a term coined by Americans to identify a different philosophy about how children learn language. This philosophy is based on theory and beliefs. It is from this philosophy that we get the whole language practice in American classrooms. To define whole language is no easy task because we are talking about theory, beliefs, and practice.

The education researchers tend to be controversial about what whole language is suppose to look like or be. In a recent publication of Educational Researchers (Vol. 19, Nov. 1990), this controversy was presented and debated. The traditionalists or people who believe in the skills approach to reading/writing and the whole language supporters both feel that whole language defies definition for very different reasons. The traditionalists are of the opinion that the whole language theorists cannot come to consensus as to how to define whole language. On the other hand, whole language theorists claim that to develop a strict, concise definition of whole language contradicts whole language philosophy because whole language is a "sociopsycholinguistic process" (Edelsky, 1990) which when defined becomes unique to each person. So, the debate goes on.

For practitioners this dilemma becomes overwhelming when one is trying to teach using a whole language approach. From whose perspective does one define whole language and practice whole language? It is difficult to answer this question because each teacher is unique with unique experiences. Therefore, one's perspective is influenced by one's experiences.

Moreover, in writing this book it became crucial that the reader understand the context in which this whole language approach emerged. In this chapter, the view of whole language will be described to assist the reader in understanding the concepts presented in this book.

Let's begin by briefly looking at the theory, beliefs, and practice of whole language as used in this book.

Learning theory has been widely researched and discussed in the educational literature. It is not the intent of this book to review all the research on learning, but rather summarize some important aspects of learning to keep in mind as one implements a whole language approach.

In Jones, Palincsar, Ogle, and Carr's book, Strategic Teaching and Learning (1987), the editors discuss some generalizations about learning based on research. They state that learning requires goal setting, that learning is influenced by development and occurs in phases, that learning involves taking new knowledge and linking it to prior knowledge, and that learning involves organizing information and developing strategies. These generalizations are a departure from the traditional way of thinking about learning which was that skill learning was the end product and that if one was presented with material in the correct hierarchy, then one would learn the material. The traditional way of thinking led to instructional materials that focused on skills in isolation and sequential step-by-step instruction of these skills. The more current generalizations put the focus of instruction on process or the developing of strategies to reach a goal. Skills are only the tools used in this process.

For whole language teachers this shift in thinking about learning is crucial. Teacher lesson plans depend on how one views learning. The literacy levels defined in this book were focused on the process of reading/writing development and the learning of strategies to become readers/writers.

Language learning has some important aspects to keep in mind. Newman (1985) reviews concisely the works of Noam Chomsky and Michael Halliday in terms of oral language development. From the whole language perspective children construct their own language and use social interaction to expand and develop their ability.

Brian Cambourne's model of learning (Cambourne, 1988) described immersion, demonstration, expectation, responsibility, use, approximation, and response as the key elements in learning. He suggests that in teaching one needs to immerse the children in literacy, demonstrate literacy, and expect the children to learn. Children need to be given the time to practice and/or use literacy, the choice in learning, an encouraging environment to take risks and approximate their learning with feedback responses to expand their learning.

Therefore, in whole language teaching it is important that daily lesson plans as well as lengthy instructional units possess the basic elements of how students learn in general and in language learning. It might be easier to think about four crucial aspects of learning: model/demonstration, interaction, support, and independence.

In oral language learning the child's environment provides the model of language. The parents talk to the child and encourage even a minimal response of cooing. This interaction becomes more complex as the child learns some words in the language and tries to communicate. The primary purpose in any language interaction is, of course, to communicate. The parent lends support by assisting the child in communicating. The child will independently use the language learned to communicate in another situation.

Let's look at these aspects in terms of reading. The teacher models the act of reading by reading together with the children. The teacher and children interact with the text to gain understanding of the author's message. The teacher's role is to support the children as they read together and encourage them to be risk takers and try reading on their own. The children, having been supported and guided in reading, will try reading independently. The same aspects hold true for writing as well and need to be included in writing experiences.

Moreover, if learning is to take place in a whole language approach, it is important that the teacher is knowledgeable about the learning theory principles. It is also important that the teacher recognizes and supports these principles in her/his teaching.

This theory is driven by the beliefs teachers have about children and their learning. Whole language teachers believe that the most important aspect in any literacy experience is the message to be communicated. The experience must be meaningful to the players. Therefore, all learning experiences should be meaningful to the children and relevant to their lives. Whole language teachers believe that children can learn to read and write as easily as they learned to speak. They also feel that reading and writing can be learned in the same manner as spoken language. Children learn from active involvement with language and construct their own meaning as they speak, listen, read, or write based on their experiences or prior knowledge.

Teachers believe that their role in teaching is one of supporter. They look for ways that they can assist and guide the children without taking away the children's ownership of learning. They believe they are responsible for providing a rich language environment in terms of literature and writing experiences for the children. They encourage children to take charge of their learning and be risk takers. The teachers work collaboratively with students to decide on curriculum for the classroom.

Beliefs actualized become classroom practices. One sees teachers reading to children, sharing reading with children, and guiding them in their reading. One sees children independently reading and writing in and out of the classroom. Children celebrate their reading and writing by sharing their work with others.

Students are actively engaged in the reading and writing process. Literature is the primary reading material and their own intentions to communicate form the basis for them in writing.

Some characteristics of a whole language classroom include:

Curiosity and inquiry, which are priorities as the class engages in learning.

Dialogue and interaction, which abound in the classroom among peers and between teacher and students.

Learning contexts, which focus on meaningful, authentic communication with real books and real writing, not contrived.

A classroom climate that is stimulating, enriched, and literate.

The cueing strategies of prior knowledge (semantic cues), knowledge of language (syntactic cues), and knowledge of print symbols, picture clues, text clues, etc. (grapho-phonemic cues), which are utilized by children to learn new words.

Daily reading and writing.

Children learning and competing with themselves, so they feel they are a successful member of the larger group.

Integration of the language arts into all content areas.

Quality literature.

Child-centered curriculum.

As stated earlier, defining whole language is not an easy task because we are looking at new dimensions in theory, beliefs of teachers, and practices of teachers. Whole language cannot be learned in one workshop or one year. It is a process of changing and refining the teacher's whole outlook on teaching and learning. The following puzzle figure attempts to display the many facets of whole language at a glance. Teachers need to take one piece at a time and work on their own knowledge and methodology of teaching and learning.

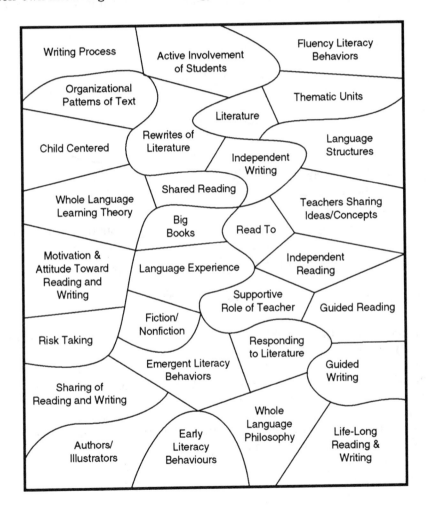

Summary

1. Learning flourishes when it is linked to prior knowledge.

2. Learning occurs in phases and is influenced by organization and strategy development.

3. Goal setting is important in learning.

4. Literacy learning is influenced by the following four aspects:

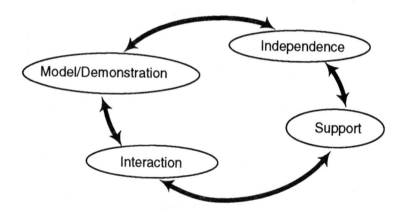

5. Teachers believe that the child is the focus of the classroom. The teacher's role is one of facilitator and supporter.

6. The whole language classroom is an active and interactive literate environment.

7. There are many factors involved in understanding whole language and these factors make up the whole of whole language.

Chapter 2   Interpreting the New Zealand Model

It's the middle of the school year in New Zealand (summer in the United States). The school that I'm about to enter has only one floor. All classrooms have two doors, one that opens into a courtyard and the other which opens onto the playground fields. As I proceed down the hall past the principal's office I notice that the outside office is decorated with large paintings by children retelling a favorite story. Other walls in the hall have countless drawings, posters, and writing pieces, all expressing the children's literature reading and content study.

I enter the classroom and at first glance I am unable to find the teacher. Finally I see her in a corner reading with a group of children. There is a great deal of activity in the room, but I get the sense that it is directed. All of the children know what they are suppose to do and cooperatively work with their peers on the tasks. One group writes a story together, discussing the content as they proceed. Another group reads their books aloud to each other. Another group examines rocks and minerals in a science center, writing down information about the items. Yet another group manipulates objects in working out math problems.

As I move from group to group I ask what their task involves. The children readily answer with all the details and procedures. Many of these tasks are ongoing and take days to complete, I am told.

Four children approach me to share their dinosaur project that they have been working on for the past week. Each student tells their part. One student is an artist and he shows his drawings to explain the project. The project was an explanation of three types of dinosaurs, where they lived, what they ate, etc. The second student reads the collaborative report on the dinosaurs. Each child had read different books on these dinosaurs and contributed this information to the report. Lastly, the children showed me a display of model dinosaurs and their habitat. I asked why they chose to do this report. They said that they were interested in dinosaurs so they did this project. It was not required. The teacher encourages these projects of interest by the children.

The classroom was alive with children's work on the walls, hanging from the ceiling, and in content subject centers. What they were studying in each subject was apparent. Books were everywhere. There were classroom libraries in several parts of the room. For example, in the social studies center, there were nonfiction and fiction books about the topic. One could feel the enthusiasm for books and learning.

It's 10:30 A.M. and time for tea. The teacher and most children leave the room. Some children remain because they are so involved with their study that they want to finish. The teacher leaves the choice up to the children. Some children go to the library which is run by the children at this time because the librarian is in the faculty room having tea. Other children go into the courtyard or playground fields to enjoy the sunny weather. These children (usually a couple of hundred) are supervised by one or two teachers. The older children play and care for the younger children. The rest of the teachers go into the faculty room for tea and chat about their teaching and children. They are relaxed and enjoy each other's companionship.

After about twenty minutes, the teachers return to their classrooms where the children are already involved in their work. The teacher may gather the children together on the rug to share a book with them before they continue with their daily tasks. After the reading, the teacher will pull together another group of children to work on reading and writing. This activity continues through the morning and afternoon. However, the teacher will gather the children together for class instruction depending on her plan for the day.

This description of a New Zealand school is not exceptional. It is common. The educational system in New Zealand is a true model of process learning and whole language as Americans define it. For this reason it is important to understand what the New Zealanders do and how Americans might use this model. It was with this in mind that I implemented the Skaneateles Language Arts Program. From this description and other observations one must realize that the New Zealand culture and American culture are very different. Some of the New Zealand ways will not work in American schools due to these differences.

Some of these differences include American achievement tests, American bureacracy, American education law, and the American tradition of the basal reader. New Zealand does not formally test their students until they are in junior or senior high school. In New Zealand the curriculum of the schools is a national curriculum. That is, each school in New Zealand is responsible to the national government for their instructional practices. The content is common across the country, which is not as culturally different as the United States.

The teachers do not have the numerous federal and state requirements or laws to constrain them in their teaching. Our paper trail is much more complex and lengthy.

The basal reader has been symptomatic of our educational system: the top-down approach. The experts (basal reader) will instruct the teacher in how s/he is to teach. The basal reader is a teacher-proof material. Any person with minimal background in teaching can use a basal reader and teach because of the format. The basal dictates when and how reading instruction will take place. The teacher can read the questions to ask to the students, instruct in skills, and assign workbook pages by merely reading the teacher's guide. These teacher-proof type of programs have found their way into other content area textbooks. Even our schools often mirror this authoritarian type of approach, that is, the mandates come from the top, down.

American schools are changing and whole language is only one aspect of this shift from traditional top-down approach to a bottom-up approach. However, the change is slow. It is difficult to eliminate all the constraints of the past to allow this change to occur. Moreover, the teacher who has been trained traditionally experiences many difficulties in transitioning, no matter how motivated. Therefore, looking to New Zealand for their demonstrations of whole language and integrating them into American schools is a great place to begin.

There are many characteristics that can be adopted from the New Zealand program.

1. **The language arts program is child-centered.** We can shift the teacher planning of all activities in the classroom to collaborative planning in a classroom. What are your children interested in learning about this year in the areas of science, social studies, etc.? These can be discussed and planned together. The teacher can offer choices and encourage the children's ownership into the curriculum. If a teacher is required to follow curriculum mandates, then the method by which one learns the topic can be planned cooperatively.

2. **The teacher's role is one of support and resource.** Oftentimes we promote dependency of our children by requiring that every decision the children make involves the teacher. What classroom procedures can I teach my children to promote independence? Can I establish a classroom routine which has the

children in an active role and me in a facilitator's role? When a crisis arises in a classroom, it is important to involve the class in the decision making. This collaboration demonstrates to the children that they have ownership in the class and that the teacher is part of that ownership, not sole authority.

3. The classroom encourages literacy and focuses on the child. How many books are displayed in my classroom? Are they enticing, motivating, and informational books? Do I encourage book talks and sharing of books? Can I keep my classroom libraries updated with books from the school library? Are there drawings, writings, and projects of students everywhere or do I have only one section with children's work? Is the classroom climate reflective of a combination of teacher and student input or is the classroom mostly the teacher's work? Do I have class responsibilities built into my class-helper system such as a helper who organizes the class library or a helper who puts up children's work?

4. The language arts are integrated into all content areas. Using the content areas to teach reading and writing is a start. It may only be one unit in each area but it helps to demonstrate to children that the language arts are tools to learning in all subjects.

5. Teachers work collaboratively with other teachers in planning, teaching, and building a school community. How often do I share my ideas with other teachers or ask for help with some area of instruction? Are there times in the school day that I can meet and plan with other teachers at my grade level? How often do I collaboratively plan a unit of study with a colleague? Do I share with my colleagues professional articles, books, and writing? Does the faculty work together as a team to benefit children? Do I include special area teachers (art, music) in my unit planning?

6. Teachers encourage the involvement of parents and other community people in their teaching.
Have I encourage my parents to come into the classroom during school hours and share in classroom activities? Do I have parent volunteers to work with children or to work on special projects? When my class becomes involved in a topic do I seek parents or other community people to come in and share their experiences to make the topic become real and meaningful? Do I have special days to cele-

brate community or family days? For example: grandparents' day, fire prevention day, special person of the week, etc.

7. The reading and writing experiences are meaningful and have a real purpose in the lives of the children.

Are my thematic units and instructional units centered around real issues? Are the tasks involved meaningful to the students? For example: The children write letters to an author they're studying to find out why he wrote about cats. One child brings in an insect and several children decide to read about this insect and report their findings to the class. Various books are provided for children to read on their literacy level about the theme for the week. A newspaper article is interesting and unique to the children and the teacher plans a unit around this topic to assist the children in learning more about it.

8. Teachers provide successful experiences in the language arts for all children regardless of needs.

All classrooms have children with varying needs. Do I provide different activities for my students so that everyone can be successful and also contribute to the theme being studied? Do children have choices in these activities and ways of accomplishing them? For example, can a low-achieving student work with a more able student on a project in which they have a mutual interest? Do children feel comfortable in suggesting new ideas or ways of doing things?

9. Children are actively involved in their daily classroom tasks.

A whole language classroom is often noisy but not chaotic. The children are talking with others but not about play. They are engaged in discussing academic issues such as how to best write the description or what a word they're reading means. Is your classroom focused on you all day? Do your children spend lengthy periods of time working on tasks without your involvement? Are you seen by your students as not only the disciplinarian, but as a resource?

10. Risk taking and mistakes are acceptable for both children and teachers.

Since we know that important ingredients in learning are risk taking and mistakes, these must be acceptable if we are to promote learning. Children who feel o.k. about making mistakes and do not lose self-esteem when a mistake is made can develop more strategies for learning and more knowledge about themselves. This is also true for teachers. If schools encourage risk taking and it's o.k. to make mistakes, then the school environment will promote teacher learning as well. New ideas will flourish and the school will move ahead.

There is much we can learn from the New Zealand model. These ideas can be adapted to fit our American schools and to work toward a more collaborative, child-centered school system. The remaining chapters of this book will try to give teachers some assistance in moving in this direction. These ideas and structures are what one school district found useful in implementing a whole language approach to the language arts.

Summary

1. New Zealand's model of language arts is whole language in practice.

2. American schools have several constraints the New Zealanders do not share. This model will require adaptation for American schools.

3. Many characteristics from New Zealand schools can be adopted here with modifications.

Chapter 3   Becoming a Whole Language Teacher

In the first two chapters the characteristics of whole language were discussed from the theoretical to the practical, from the New Zealand to American perspectives. In this chapter we will examine what you are already doing that is "whole language" and what areas you may want to work on changing.

As a teacher you will be going through several changes as you make the transition into whole language. You may already have moved through several stages already. How do you feel about whole language? How comfortable are you with the changes? The following chart was adapted from the work of Rutherford, Hall, and Newlove (1982). This chart will indicate to you where you are in your use of the innovation of whole language. In other words, how comfortable you are with whole language. Level 6 means you have enough confidence with the concepts to develop your own ideas and share them with others. Level 1 means that you are just beginning and are looking for information to make the change. Select one level which most closely describes your feelings at the moment.

Levels of Use of Whole Language Chart

	Level	Description
6.	Refocusing	In using whole language, I have some ideas about something that would work even better.
5.	Collaboration	I am concerned about relating what I am doing with what other teachers are doing.
4.	Consequence	How is my use of whole language affecting the students?

3. Management   I seem to be spending all my time in getting material ready.

2. Personal   How will using whole language affect me?

1. Informational   I would like to know more about whole language.

0. Awareness   I am not concerned about or interested in whole language.

This chart is also useful as you utilize each change in whole language. For example, if you are beginning to use shared reading for the first time, then you are probably at level 1 or 2. As you progress in your change you will continue to move up the levels until you are in the position to be developing and presenting ideas about shared reading on your own. It's a handy chart to check yourself as you transition into whole language and also to realize that change is a process and will take time. Some teachers take years to move from one level to another. Others move from one level to another in a couple of weeks. However, the important thing to keep in mind is that we all have similar feelings and questions as we transition.

Now that you have determined your feelings about whole language, what areas should you focus on? What areas do you already have working for you? The following exercise will help you to realize where you are in whole language teaching.

There are seven (7) areas of whole language listed: Classroom Organization, Classroom Instruction, Resources, Assessment, Record Keeping, Communication, and Professional Development of the Teacher. In each of these areas there is a description of how you would be functioning in these areas if you were a novice whole language teacher, developing whole language teacher, and skilled whole language teacher. Read each description for each area. Select the category which most closely fits your practice at this time. Put a check next to it. These selections can be charted at the end.

1. CLASSROOM ORGANIZATION

Novice Whole Language Teacher

Furniture is arranged to promote (1 to 2 of these):

> peer collaboration
> group sharing and/or instruction
> small group work (activity centers)
> individual conferencing
> project work
> classroom library
> supplies for reading and writing

Developing Whole Language Teacher

Furniture is arranged to promote (3 to 4 of these):

> peer collaboration
> group sharing and/or instruction
> small group work (activity centers)
> individual conferencing
> project work
> classroom library
> supplies for reading and writing

Skilled Whole Language Teacher

Furniture is arranged to promote all of these:

> peer collaboration
> group sharing and/or instruction
> small group work (activity centers)
> individual conferencing
> project work
> classroom library
> supplies for reading & writing

2. CLASSROOM INSTRUCTION

a. Read To

Novice Whole Language Teacher

Class is read to 2 or 3 times per week
from a book generally at random.

Developing Whole Language Teacher

Class is read to on an almost daily basis
from a book selected generally on teacher
and/or student interests.

Skilled Whole Language Teacher

Class is read to on a daily basis without exception

from a book chosen by teacher and/or children;
this selection is based on classroom objectives
and integrated with other subject areas.

b. Language Experience (Grs. Preschool-1)

Novice Whole Language Teacher

Teacher selects individual students
once a month to dictate a story and
does a group experience story several
times a week.

Developing Whole Language Teacher

Teacher selects individual students twice a
month to dictate a story and does a group
experience story twice a week.

Skilled Whole Language Teacher

Teacher selects individual students weekly
to dictate a story and does a group
experience story once or twice a month.

c. Shared Reading

Novice Whole Language Teacher

Big books/books are read together with entire class

and generally as the teacher sees skills in
the text, they are taught.

Developing Whole Language Teacher

Big books/books are read together with entire class
and the teacher prepares her skills to teach
from the text before reading.

Skilled Whole Language Teacher

Big books/books are selected and used which
correlate directly to the objectives of the
class instruction and at the specific level
of literacy development of the class.

d. Guided Reading

Novice Whole Language Teacher

Students are taught in small groups based
upon designated literacy levels only; there
is limited movement between groups.

Developing Whole Language Teacher

Students are taught in small groups
based upon determined literacy level; there
is some flexible grouping for skills.

Skilled Whole Language Teacher

Students are taught in flexible small groups
at their literacy level or according to
skill needs, which is determined by the teacher
in her/his use of running records,* classroom observation,
and/or checklists.

e. Independent Reading

Novice Whole Language Teacher

Children are given time to read books
independently 2 to 3 times per week and
children list the books read;
children select books on own but often not
appropriately for literacy level.

Developing Whole Language Teacher

Children are given time to read books
independently several times a week; the teacher
guides the children in the selection through demonstration;
students list books and respond to them in some fashion;
mini lessons* are given for skill areas and
conferencing is tried.

* See Glossary

Skilled Whole Language Teacher

Children are given time to read books
independently on a daily basis; the teacher
guides the children in the selection through demonstration
and mini lessons; students list
books and respond to them meaningfully
in the form of response logs;
mini lessons are planned around skill need;
individual conferencing is done weekly for each
student and skill work is developed.

f. Writing

Novice Whole Language Teacher

Children are given time to write on their own topics
2 to 3 times per week; teacher instructs with some
mini lessons and guides them in their writing by
conferencing occasionally; teacher-directed topics
are often written.

Developing Whole Language Teacher

Children are given time to write on their
own topics several times a week; the teacher uses
some conferencing to determine skill needs;
mini lessons are done before each independent writing
 session; teacher begins to develop guided writing activities
to expand her/his students' writing ability.

Skilled Whole Language Teacher

Daily, children are given time to write on their own
topics; mini lessons and conferencing are part of each
independent writing session; individual conferencing is done
weekly for each student and skill work is developed; teacher
develops guided writing activities as determined by class
needs.

3. RESOURCES

a. Classroom Library Books

Novice Whole Language Teacher

Classroom library books are available;
books are randomly arranged.

Developing Whole Language Teacher

Several classroom library books are available
at various literacy levels, genre, and subject
content; books are generally arranged according
to topics or genre.

Skilled Whole Language Teacher

Multiple copies of library books at various
literacy levels, genres, and subject content are available;
books are arranged and organized into various literacy
levels within the genres or topics.

b. Classroom Sets/Big Books

Novice Whole Language Teacher

Teacher selects books for novelty
or interest value.

Developing Whole Language Teacher

Teacher begins to select books to use in
accordance with interest and some determined
needs of class.

Skilled Whole Language Teacher

Teacher selects and uses books in coordination
with literacy levels of students, interest of students,
and specific learning outcomes set by the teacher for
her/his class.

c. Individual Books

Novice Whole Language Teacher

Students select their own books based upon
their own criteria; the teacher begins to assist
students in their selection of appropriate books
for literacy level and interests.

Developing Whole Language Teacher

Students are taught how to select appropriate books at their literacy level and for part of the time they utilize it; teacher assists in selection.

Skilled Whole Language Teacher

Students select appropriately their own books; teacher guides students in developing a wide variety of books for reading.

4.   ASSESSMENT

Novice Whole Language Teacher

Teachers begin to become familiar with and use 1 or 2 of the following:

> teacher observation
> running records
> benchmarks for literacy levels*
> checklists
> conferencing
> response journals
> writing pieces
> language arts portfolio*

*See Glossary

Developing Whole Language Teacher

Teachers begin to become familiar with
and use 3 or 4 of the following:

> teacher observation
> running records
> benchmarks for literacy levels
> checklists
> conferencing
> response journals
> writing pieces
> language arts portfolio

Skilled Whole Language Teacher

Teachers begin to become familiar with
and use all of the following:

> teacher observation
> running records
> benchmarks for literacy levels
> checklists
> conferencing
> response journals
> writing pieces
> language arts portfolio

5.   RECORD KEEPING

Novice Whole Language Teacher

Teachers develop systems of

management and keep records for
4 or 5 of the following:

> number of books read by student
> responses student writes to literature
> number of writing pieces written
>   by student
> writing development in pieces
> skill work done in reading and writing
> conferences held
> mini lessons completed
> shared books read and purposes
> guided reading groups and progress
> where class is on any one day
>   in independent reading /writing
> benchmarks for literacy levels
> focus units completed with purposes
> genre and content instructed
> books read to class and purposes
> overall development in reading
>   and writing process

Developing Whole Language Teacher

Teachers develop systems of
management and keep records for
6 or 10 of the following:

> number of books read by student
> responses student writes to literature
> number of writing pieces written
>   by student
> writing development in pieces
> skill work done in reading and writing
> conferences held

    mini lessons completed
shared books read and purposes
guided reading groups and progress
where class is on any one day
   in independent reading /writing
benchmarks for literacy levels
focus units completed with purposes
genre and content instructed
books read to class and purposes
overall development in reading
   and writing process

Skilled Whole Language Teacher

Teachers develop systems of
management and keep records for
all of the following:

    number of books read by student
responses student writes to literature
number of writing pieces written by student
writing development in pieces
skill work done in reading and writing
conferences held
mini lessons completed
shared books read and purposes
guided reading groups and progress
where class is on any one day
   in independent reading /writing
benchmarks for literacy levels
focus units completed with purposes
genre and content instructed
books read to class and purposes
overall development in reading
   and writing process

6. COMMUNICATION

Novice Whole Language Teacher

Teacher attempts to explain and share how
whole language works in her classroom to:
colleagues, administration, parents;
teacher joins a support group.

Developing Whole Language Teacher

Teacher is able to explain and share how
whole language works in her classroom to:
colleagues, administration, parents;
teacher begins to assist other teachers
in whole language; teacher is an active member
of a whole language support group.

Skilled Whole Language Teacher

Teacher confidently explains and shares how
whole language works in her classroom to:
colleagues, administration, parents;
teacher supports other teachers in whole language;
teacher can lead presentations and discussions on
whole language for her peers.

7. PROFESSIONAL DEVELOPMENT OF THE TEACHER

Novice Whole Language Teacher

Teacher has read 1 or 2 books
relating to whole language.

Developing Whole Language Teacher

Teacher has read 3 or 4 books on whole language;
reads journal articles occasionally;
has attended 1 inservice or graduate course on
whole language.

Skilled Whole Language Teacher

Teacher has read several books on whole language;
reads journal articles often;
attends regularly inservice or graduate courses on
whole language; writes on whole language for other teachers.

Decision Chart

Check type of teacher where description is most like you for each area.

Area	Novice	Developing	Skilled
1. Classroom Organization			
2. Classroom Instruction a. Read To			
b. Language Experience (PS-1)			
c. Shared Reading			
d. Guided Reading			
e. Independent Reading			
f. Writing			

Area	Novice	Developing	Skilled
3. Resources a. Classroom Library Books			
b. Classroom Sets/ Big Books			
c. Individual Books			
4. Assessment			
5. Record Keeping			
6. Communication			
7. Professional Development			

These two charts will assist you in assessing where you are in whole language and what you need to become more familiar with in your pursuit of whole language. Now you are ready to begin or further the process of becoming a whole language teacher. The next chapter will help you decide where to begin and how to begin.

Summary

1. Becoming a whole language teacher is a process and can take a long time. First, one must understand where one is in the change process.

2. There are several aspects to whole language teaching. Identifying what one has already attained and what one needs to change can be helpful in the transition to whole language teaching.

Chapter 4 Starting Out in Whole Language

In the previous chapters you have read about what whole language is and some identifiable characteristics. You have also tried to identify some specifics of whole language that you already practice and those about which you need to learn more. But how do you start? The answer is simple. Start from where you are and plan what you will do next. Each teacher is at a different starting point and this fact is significant. In addition, all schools and school districts are different. We are all working under constraints which will hinder us but in different ways. We need to recognize them and see what can be done to overcome them.

Let's start with you. Where did you place yourself on the levels of use chart (Chapter 3)? Did you place yourself above level 3? If you did, then you may want to tackle a large segment of the unknown aspects of whole language. You have the confidence and background to take a big leap. If you are only using literature, then you will want to refine your reading/writing development structure with the literacy levels (See Chapters 9-14).

However, if you placed yourself at level 3 or lower, you may want to read more books and articles on whole language. Try a few activities and see if they work for you. You're probably still using the basal and will want to try to change more of your classroom structure to fit the whole language components. These components are described and explained with activities in Chapter 6.

Take a look at your present teaching. What do you already practice that is within the whole language philosophy? Perhaps you read to children or have the children silently read everyday. Maybe you use the writing process or have children keep journals. All of these activities are important to list. For one thing, the list makes you feel that you have already begun and have a shorter way to go. It also helps you to categorize which areas you need to change. Does your present language arts program have more writing aspects of whole language than reading? Are you reading literature but don't know what strategies to teach?

After you've listed the aspects you know and use, list the aspects you want to try next. For example, I want to learn about running records. Then, list any constraints that might be preventing you from moving ahead. Next, list the possible solutions or where to investigate this aspect. For example:

Whole Language Aspect To Try	Constraints	Possible Solutions
Running records	1. Resource person to assess my progress	1. Check with reading teacher
	2. Time in day to use;	2. Use reading group time once a week
	3. Reaction of parents to new activity	3. In classroom newsletter to parents explain running record and ask for volunteers to come in during this activity to lead independent activities with other children

This same procedure can be used with each of the area topics from Chapter 3: Classroom Organization, Classroom Instruction, Resources, Assessment, Record Keeping, Communication, and Professional Development. It might be helpful to select one or two items from each area to work on in the next school year. Taking on too many areas will only cause frustration and the feeling of not being successful.

Here are some other helpful suggestions for transitioning to whole language teaching:

1. It is important that you have the support and acceptance of your colleagues and principal when attempting to change to whole language. Keep your colleagues and principal informed of your ideas and work out the constraints with them. They may be excellent resources to you.

2. Join a whole language support group in the area or form one in your school with others who want to try whole language. The support is important when you are frustrated by an obstacle. The support group is also important to the process of whole language teaching.

Whole language teaching is a collaborative process in the classroom: Teacher and students work together with the curriculum. Teachers also need to work with other teachers in sharing concepts, understandings, and activities. It is not a close-the-door-do-your-own-thing teaching style. Working in cooperative groups in your school to plan units for whole language expands your resource for ideas.

The support people should be people you trust and can work with for the benefit of children. You will want to feel accepted in the support group and not afraid of sharing mistakes as well as successes. The support group will want everyone to feel that their ideas can be accepted or criticized openly without hurt feelings. Your support group will be helpful to you if they are honest and trusting.

3. Begin small and expand as the momentum gets going. Too many teachers in starting whole language want to dismiss all that they've done for years and start with everything new. This notion can be dangerous. Rejecting all of what you've done in teaching to date leaves you without any structure or safety net. There is no one right way to teach using whole language, but rather, many different perspectives as one moves through the change process. There is also the fact that teachers have individual learning styles of their own and need to be recognized in this process. No two teachers will teach or change to whole language in the same way. Reviewing the learning theory, we see that if learning is to take place, then we build on prior knowledge. You already have much knowledge in the area of teaching. Use this knowledge to build a new concept of teaching.

4. Students have a role in your changing classroom. Reflect with the students on completed activities. Which activities worked well and which activities need refinement? Ask for their input as to why it did or didn't work. Discuss ways of improving it. This is an opportunity for children to develop ownership and responsibility in the classroom.

5. In order to know when and what succeeded or failed, it might be helpful to keep a log or diary. In this log you can list the activities or concepts that you've tried. Then you can reflect on the activity and how it could be improved or what went well for future use.

For example: Suppose you wanted to start an independent writing time. You might list that the procedures went well until you found out that conferencing with students was taking too long. Most children only met with you once every two weeks. You decided to try group conferencing and conferencing by walking around to the children. After trying this for a few weeks you found that you met with the children more often and had a better feel for their work.

These log entries can also show your progress and serve as helpful hints to teachers trying the same idea.

6. In the selection of ideas, concepts, or activities to try in whole language, it is most important to know why you're doing the task, providing the experience, or teaching the strategy. Whole language, unlike the basal reader, does not come with a teacher's manual which lists the reasons and purposes for the instruction. These purposes in whole language are the result of the teacher's assessed needs of her/his students and a planned activity to encourage the students' development in literacy. In order to be able to do this, the teacher needs to have an understanding of the literacy levels and be able to assess the needs of her/his students.

7. Learning whole language teaching theory and methods is never ending, just as no one stops learning in life. We experience changes but the learning doesn't stop. Therefore, realize that this is just the beginning of your learning about whole language. There will be many more years to come.

Summary

1. It's important to have a plan in starting out in whole language teaching. The change can't happen instantly. It takes time.

2. The plan should include where you are and what you are already doing in whole language. Next, it should list the areas you want to focus on in teaching. Lastly, the constraints need to be worked out in order to proceed.

3. Several suggestions are recommended in starting out, including move slowly, keep what you do that is successful and add on the new, join a support group, and know your purpose for the task.

Chapter 5 Goals for Whole Language Teaching

Many teachers find goal setting important in their classrooms when using the whole language approach. In the basal approach the goal setting was easy. One knew that the students had to complete Book A before going on to Book B and pass the end of book tests. In whole language the structure can be vague for those teachers starting out and those who don't have the reading/writing strategies and behaviors at their fingertips. This chapter is an attempt to assist teachers who are becoming whole language teachers in goal setting for their programs.

The first set of learning outcomes are understandings and attitudes teachers would want to observe in their students at the end of the elementary years. These end goals seem to be helpful in placing some of the methods and practices of whole language into proper perspective. For example, a first grade teacher would not want to have as a grade level goal: children responding to text by writing a paragraph about the book and their own experiences. This type of goal, while important to literacy development, is not appropriate for first graders.

The second part of the learning outcomes is what would typically be expected for third graders to demonstrate. Some of these learning outcomes have "Shared and Guided Reading" or other whole language component parts written next to them. This indicates that third grade students would not be able to demonstrate these outcomes independently but would be able to demonstrate them with the support of the teacher in Shared or Guided Reading.

LEARNING OUTCOMES OF ELEMENTARY STUDENTS

ATTITUDES

- Enjoys reading and writing independently and with peers

- Independently selects own reading books and writing topics

- Is self-confident about literacy work and shares enthusiastically with others

- Initiates reading and writing without prompting

AUTHOR UNDERSTANDINGS

- Understands that authors are people who write books

- Can locate on each book the author's name

- Can identify similar aspects of authors' styles (language used, sentence structure, characters, plot, setting, mood, form, genre, etc.)

- Can compare and contrast authors in terms of style, theme, intent, background, etc.

- Can mimic an author in own writing in terms of style, theme, intent, etc.

- Understands that authors go through a lengthy writing process in the development of a book

ILLUSTRATOR UNDERSTANDINGS

- Can locate on each book the illustrator or determine that one is not indicated/doesn't exist

- Can identify similar aspects of illustrators' styles (theme, mood, drawing or painting aspects, etc.)

- Can determine the relationship between illustrations and written text

- Understands that illustrations can and do tell the story or enhance it

READING STRATEGIES

- Can identify a book, a newspaper, a magazine, piece of paper, etc. as different items

- Can hold book in appropriate position for reading

- Can identify the parts of the book (author/illustrator, table of contents, chapters, page numbers, illustrations etc.)

- Can move through a book while reading appropriately (left to right, return sweep, left page before right page, top before bottom)

- Can utilize illustrations in book to enhance text meaning

- Can use semantic cues while reading (meaning)

- Can use syntactic cues while reading (language structure)

- Can use phonetic cues while reading (sound/symbol)
- Able to integrate cueing strategies while reading

- Understands which cueing strategies are necessary when reading unfamiliar words

- Can understand what the author is saying literally at level

- Can understand what the author means at literacy level

- Can relate what author writes to own experiences and apply in own life at literacy level

- Can identify the genre being read by appropriate characteristics

- Can read for a variety of purposes

WRITING STRATEGIES

- Can identify letters of the alphabet by name (capital and lower case)

- Can form letters of the alphabet appropriately

- Can write using appropriate punctuation, capitalization, and spelling

- Can compose in various genres

- Can compose in various styles and for a variety of purposes

- Can compose interesting writing pieces with appropriate organization and sentence variety

- Can select own topic and write independently

- Can write appropriately and creatively on given topic

- Uses the components of the writing process (prewriting, drafting, revising, editing, and publishing) to compose

RESPONSE

- Can orally respond to literature by explaining the main idea or theme

- Can orally respond by summarizing the main events of literature piece

- Can orally give the details of the piece of literature

- Can express own feelings about literature and relate it to own life

- Can criticize and/or evaluate piece of literature based upon own life experiences and literary aspects (genre, style, theme,language usage, etc.) — oral and written response

- Can write a response to literature by explaining the main idea or theme

- Can write a response by summarizing the main events of literature piece

- Can write the details of the piece of literature

- Can express in writing own feelings about literature
  and relate it to own life

UNDERSTANDINGS OF LITERARY ELEMENTS

- Able to identify major and minor characters

- Can develop character profile from text

- Able to identify and summarize plot

- Can identify climax and show sequence of events before
  and after for support

- Understands problem and resolution in piece

- Can identify and support theme, mood, purpose

- Understands organization and structure — can support view

- Identifies general setting and understands shifts in settings

SHARING

- Has self-confidence and pride in sharing work both reading
  and written

- Can read with appropriate oral expression reading or
  writing material

- Can accept and give constructive feedback about work and integrate it into piece

- Can defend piece from own point of view with reasonable support

USE OF LANGUAGE ARTS IN CONTENT AREAS

- Able to gather information from a variety of resources

- Uses note-taking skills effectively

- Able to use gathered information to write a report in various styles (factual report, narrative report, personification report, etc.)

- Able to decide which resources are appropriate to gain information

- Able to use a variety of resources effectively

- Can evaluate resources as to validity for information

- Can read content area material with understanding

- Can integrate content area material with prior knowledge and apply new knowledge

The following is a profile of the learning outcomes one would have of a child completing grade 3.

END OF GRADE 3

ATTITUDES

- **Generally** enjoys reading and writing independently and with peers

- **Often** independently selects own reading books and writing topics

- **Becoming** self-confident about literacy work and shares enthusiastically with others

- **Often** initiates reading and writing without prompting

AUTHOR UNDERSTANDINGS

- Understands that authors are people who write books

- Can locate on each book the author

- Can identify similar aspects of authors' styles (language used, sentence structure, characters, plot, setting, mood, form, genre, etc.) **Shared & Guided Reading mostly**

- Can compare and contrast authors in terms of style, theme, intent, background, etc. **Shared & Guided Reading mostly**

- Can mimic an author in own writing in terms of style, theme, intent, etc. **Guided writing mostly**

- Beginning to understand that authors go through a lengthy writing process in the development of a book

ILLUSTRATOR UNDERSTANDINGS

- Can locate on each book the illustrator or determine that one is not indicated/doesn't exist

- Can identify similar aspects of illustrators' styles (theme, mood, drawing or painting aspects, etc.) **Shared & Guided Reading**

- Can determine the relationship between illustrations and written text **Shared & Guided Reading**

- Understands that illustrations can and do tell the story or enhance it

READING STRATEGIES

- Can identify a book, a newspaper, a magazine, piece of paper, etc. as different items

- Can hold book in appropriate position for reading

- Can identify the parts of the book (author/illustrator, table of contents, chapters, page numbers, illustrations, etc.)

- Can move through a book while reading appropriately (left to right, return sweep, left page before right page, top before bottom)

- Can utilize illustrations in book to enhance text meaning

- Can use semantic cues while reading (meaning)

- Can use syntactic cues while reading (language structure)

- Can use phonetic cues while reading (sound/symbol)

- Able to integrate cueing strategies while reading

- Understands which cueing strategies are necessary when reading unfamiliar words

- Can understand what the author is saying literally at literacy level

- Can understand what the author means at literacy level

- Can relate what author writes to own experiences and apply in own life at literacy level

- Can identify the genre being read by appropriate characteristics **Shared & Guided Reading** mostly

- Can read for a variety of purposes **Shared & Guided Reading mostly**

WRITING STRATEGIES

- Can identify letters of the alphabet by name (capital and lower case)

- Can form letters of the alphabet appropriately

- Can write using appropriate punctuation, capitalization, and spelling **Most of the time but not mastered**

- Can compose in various genres **Guided Writing mostly**

- Can compose in various styles and for a variety of purposes **Guided Writing mostly**

- Can compose interesting writing pieces with appropriate organization and sentence variety **Some in Guided Writing**

- Can often select own topic and write independently

- Can often write appropriately and creatively on given topic

- Uses the components of the writing process (prewriting, drafting, revising, editing, and publishing) to compose

RESPONSE

- Can orally respond to literature by explaining the main idea or theme

- Can orally respond by summarizing the main events of
literature piece

- Can orally give the details of the piece of literature

- Can express own feelings about literature and relate it to
own life **Orally mostly**

- Can criticize and/or evaluate piece of literature
based upon own life experiences and literary aspects
(genre, style, theme, language usage, etc.) — oral
and written response **Orally in Shared
and Guided Reading**

- Can **often** write a response to literature by explaining the
main idea or theme

- Can **often** write a response by summarizing the main
events of literature piece

- Can **often** write the details of the piece of literature

- Can **often** express in writing own feelings about
literature and relate it to own life

UNDERSTANDINGS OF LITERARY ELEMENTS

- Able to identify major and minor characters

- Can develop character profile from text **Shared Reading**

- Able to identify plot

- Can identify climax

- Identifies problem and resolution in piece

- Can identify and support theme, mood, purpose **Shared Reading**

- Understands organization and structure **Shared Reading**

- Identifies general setting

SHARING

- **Frequently** has self-confidence and pride in sharing work both reading and written

- Can **often** read with appropriate oral expression reading or writing material

- Can listen to constructive feedback about work and attempt to use it in piece

- Can give simple feedback to others about writing piece

USE OF LANGUAGE ARTS IN CONTENT AREAS

- Able to use gathered information to write a report **Guided Writing**

- Able to use a variety of resources **Shared Reading**

- Can read content area material with understanding
Shared Reading

- Can integrate content area material with prior knowledge
and apply new knowledge **Shared Reading**

Some teachers find the above listing too difficult to interpret for their specific grade level and prefer to have goals listed similar to the traditional format of scope and sequence charts. However, in whole language philosophy there is a conflict with this approach.

Whole language philosophy believes that learning is a process and is not hierarchical. Therefore, in attempting to keep within the whole language philosophy and also to assist teachers in transitioning from traditional to whole language philosophy, the following grade level guidelines were used. These charts represent what an average grade level student would demonstrate. They are meant to be used as guidelines only. Teachers need to assess their own students' needs and set goals for their own students in terms of their capabilities.

Language Arts Guidelines for Preschool

Understanding the Story

Orally retells what the read aloud story was about

Orally discusses what was liked best about the story

Often remembers and repeats a rhythmical or repetitive phrase from story

Parts of the Story

Identifies what event happened at the beginning and end of the story

Recognizes where the title of the story is located

Often asks questions about parts of the story to clarify the meaning

Understanding About Books

Understands what a book is and that reading aloud brings the story to life

Enjoys having books read aloud and often selects the same books to be read over and over again

Understands that interaction with the story reader and the book is interesting and fun

Language Arts Guidelines for Preschool

Pronouncing Words	*Writing*	*Spelling / Grammar*
Learns some new speaking vocabulary from books and wants to use the new words	Likes to scribble to imitate adult writing	Spelling is not applicable at this level
Asks questions about some unfamiliar words for clarification	Colors pictures in an attempt to express self	Supporting and assisting children to be understandable in their speaking language is focused on at this level
Points to some words that have significance to child and will repeat them	Attempts to draw own picture of something as directed by teacher	

Language Arts Guidelines for Preschool

Assessment	Methods	Materials
Teacher observation of oral language development and book familiarity	Oral language development activities	Read To Books with simple plots
	Read To*	Oral language development activities
Anecdotal records of child's development	Language Experience*	Teacher-developed activities for reading and writing experiences
		*See Glossary

Language Arts Guidelines for Kindergarten

All Preschool behaviors and strategies are reviewed and reinforced throughout the school year.

Understanding the Story

Orally retells events from read aloud story

Remembers some details of read aloud story

Predicts what will come next in a story

Recognizes the problem in a story

Orally discusses what was liked about the story and why

Parts of the Story

Identifies that a story has a beginning and an end

Identifies the title, author, and simple plot of a story

Recognizes the main characters of the story

Understanding About Books

Understands how a book is read (where to start and how to read)

Enjoys being read to and listens attentively

Enjoys talking about books

Asks to be read to

Recognizes that books are different in illustrations as well as message

Understands that books can be reread and the message remains the same

Language Arts Guidelines for Kindergarten

Pronouncing Words	*Writing*	*Spelling / Grammar*
Learns that meaning is a priority in reading	Writes a phrase or sentence	Words are difficult to read because they are represented by letters which may or may not correspond to words
Learns to recognize words in print	Writes letters to represent words	
Learns that letters make up words and sounds	Likes to see spoken words written down by teacher (language experience)	
Recognizes most of the letters of the alphabet and the sounds of the letters		

Language Arts Guidelines for Kindergarten

Assessment	*Methods*	*Materials*
Teacher observation	Read To	Big books (published or teacher made)
Literacy levels assessments	Shared Reading*	
	Language Experience	Teacher-developed activities for reading and writing experiences
Student's writing	Some Guided Reading*	
Portfolio of language arts work (See Chapter 17)	Writing experiences	Guided reading books
	Teacherassisted reading/writing activities	
	Phonemic awareness* or segmentation activities	
		*See Glossary

Language Arts Guidelines for Grade 1

All Kindergarten behaviors and strategies are reviewed and reinforced throughout the school year.

Understanding the Story

Orally retells sequence of story events

Remembers details of story and can complete a cloze exercise*

Predicts what will come next in a story

Orally compares two aspects of a story

Identifies the problem in a story

Orally discusses what was liked about the story and why

*See Glossary

Parts of the Story

Identifies that a story has a beginning, a middle, and an end

Identifies the title, author, and simple plot of a story

Recognizes the main characters of the story

Understanding About Books

Understands how a book is read (where to start and how to read)

Enjoys being read to and listens with comprehension

Enjoys talking about books, authors, and illustrators

Recognizes that illustrators have characteristics and identifies the work of an illustrator

Recognizes that books are different in illustrations as well as in message

Language Arts Guidelines for Grade 1

Pronouncing Words

Learns that meaning is a priority in reading

Understands that words must make sense in the structure of the sentence

Uses initial consonants, final consonants, and shape of the word to figure out unfamiliar words

Learns about short and long vowels (a,e,i,o,u) , r-controlled vowels (or,ar, ur, er, ir), and blends and digraphs (bl, gl, tr, th, sh, etc.) to figure out new words

Learns words without sounding them out from memory (sight vocabulary)

Learns about contractions, compound words, and adding endings to words

Writing

Writes a story of more than one sentence

Attempts to write all parts of a sentence

Usually writes sentences with mainly one type of structure (I like...)

Likes to rewrite a familiar book with own words

Spelling / Grammar

Words are generally written in inventive spelling with many letters corresponding to the appropriate letter

Writes simple sentences

Mostly uses ending punctuation in writing but is not always accurate

Capitalization at beginning of sentences used frequently

Language Arts Guidelines for Grade 1

Assessment	*Methods*	*Materials*
Teacher observation	Read To	Literature class sets
Literacy levels assessments	Shared Reading	Teacher-developed or published activities for behavior/strategy development of reading and writing
Student's writing	Language Experience	
Running records*	Guided Reading	
Cloze exercise	Independent Reading*	Guided reading books
Portfolio of language arts work (See Chapter 17)	Guided Writing*	Individual writing dictionary
	Independent Writing	Journal/logs for writing
		Activities for literacy levels

*See Glossary

Language Arts Guidelines for Grade 2

All Grade 1 behaviors and strategies are reviewed and reinforced throughout the school year.

Understanding the Story

Responds to story by writing sequence of story events

Remembers details of story and can complete a cloze exercise

Finds the main idea in a story

Predicts what will come next in a story

Orally compares two aspects of a story

Identifies the problem in a story and how it was resolved

Responds, in writing, to a story by expressing what was liked in the story

Parts of the Story

Identifies beginning, middle, and end

Identifies the title, author, characters and their attributes, setting, problem/resolution, and simple plot of a story

Understanding About Books

Understands the parts of books (title page, table of contents, chapters, glossary, index, etc.)

Enjoys being read to and starts to read independently

Enjoys talking about books, authors, and illustrators

Recognizes that authors/illustrators have characteristics and identifies the work of authors/illustrators

Language Arts Guidelines for Grade 2

Pronouncing Words

Uses the meaning and the sentence to help figure out words

Learns about the double vowels (ex: ou, au, oo) and often uses them in decoding unfamiliar words

Applies the short and long vowels, r-controlled vowels, and blends and digraphs in figuring out new words

Knows many words without sounding them out and is rapidly picking up new ones

Prefix and suffix (ex: ly, re, pre, ness) meanings are introduced for application in understanding the author's message

Writing

Writes a story using several sentences on the same topic

Usually has all the parts of a sentence included

Often writes sentences with different structures

Likes to copy the style of a book

Attempts to revise sometimes in writing

Attempts to edit writing with teacher encouragement

Spelling / Grammar

Uses inventive spelling mostly but several words are conventionally spelled

Uses mostly correct grammar in writing

Writes simple varied sentences

Uses punctuation and capitalization in writing but is not always accurate

Language Arts Guidelines for Grade 2

Assessment	*Methods*	*Materials*
Teacher observation	Read To	Literature class sets
Literacy level assessments	Shared Reading	Teacher-developed or published activities for behavior/strategy development of reading and writing
Student's writing	Guided Reading	
	Independent Reading	
Running records	Guided Writing	Guided reading books
Cloze exercises	Independent Writing	
Teacher assessment of writing, spelling, grammar, and language use		Individual writing dictionary
		Journal/logs for writing and responding to literature
Portfolio of language arts work		Activities for literacy levels

Language Arts Guidelines for Grade 3

All Grade 2 behaviors and strategies are reviewed and reinforced throughout the school year.

Understanding the Story	*Parts of the Story*	*Understanding About Books*
Responds to story by writing sequence of story events	Identifies beginning, middle, and end	Enjoys reading independently
Recognizes description in a story	Identifies, in writing, the title, author, characters, plot, setting, type of story (genre), problem/resolution, and climax	Enjoys sharing books with peers
Finds the main idea in a story		Recognizes authors' type of writing by orally comparing stories
Recognizes cause and effect in a story		
Recognizes comparison and contrast in a story		
States, in writing, the problem and resolution of a story		
Responds, in writing, to a story by expressing own experiences relating to the story		

Language Arts Guidelines for Grade 3

Pronouncing Words

Consistently uses the meaning and the sentence to figure out words

Applies sound/symbol when necessary in figuring out words

Has extensive sight vocabulary

Applies prefixes, suffixes (ex: ly, re, pre, ness), roots, etc. in assisting with interpretation of author's message

Writing

Writes a story with beginning, middle, and end

Uses description in story

Uses correct sentence structure in story

Varies sentence structure in writing

Can write a short description of a character with detail

Edits stories for beginning capitalization and ending punctuation

Revises stories to include beginning, middle, and end

Spelling / Grammar

Uses conventional spelling often

Uses inventive spelling of all unfamiliar words so that it is readable

Writes grammatically correct sentence

Writes more complex sentences

Generally uses correct punctuation and capitalization in writing

Language Arts Guidelines for Grade 3

Assessment	Methods	Materials
Teacher observation	Read To	Literature class sets
Literacy levels assessments	Shared Reading	Teacher-developed or published activities for behavior/strategy development of reading and writing
	Guided Reading	
Student's writing	Independent Reading	
Cloze exercises	Guided Writing	Guided reading books
Running records	Independent Writing	Individual writing dictionary
Response journal or log (See Chapter 6 Independent Reading)		Journal/logs for writing and responding to literature
Portfolio of language arts work (See Chapter 17)		Activities for literacy levels

Since whole language teachers do not use teacher manuals to determine the curriculum goals for the school year, these two different approaches might be most useful when used together. The following procedure describes a method for incorporating both approaches and a means for assessment of the language arts curriculum.

The integrated plan for teachers in goal setting could be to:

1. Read and understand the learning outcomes for elementary students.

2. Assess your class as a whole in each area and list the general strengths and weaknesses for each area. Making a chart of the assessed areas might be helpful.

3. Read and understand the Guidelines for Language Arts for your grade level.

4. Assess your class in each area and list the results in terms of strengths and weaknesses. Put these additional areas on the chart and/or list them under similar areas of the learning outcomes.

5. Using this chart, develop your class learning outcomes or goals for the school year.

6. At various times throughout the school year these goals can be reassessed based on your class' progress.

7. Individual goals for students can also be assessed in this way. However, determining the literacy level of your students will assist in the

Reading and Writing Strategies areas.(See
Chapter 14)

This chart and periodic assessments will assist you as the classroom teacher in promoting literacy. It can also provide information to children, parents, and administrators on progress in the language arts.

Summary

In this chapter an overview of learning outcomes for elementary students was presented in detail. Guidelines for language arts were also presented for preschool to grade 3. These two overviews might be helpful to the whole language teacher as s/he plans the school year goals.

Chapter 6 Understanding the Listening, Speaking, Reading, and Writing Components in a Whole Language Classroom

In Chapter 5 guidelines for setting goals in your language arts curriculum as determined by class needs was discussed. The next hurdle to jump over is what does day to day practice look like and how do you use your goals in this process. This chapter will explain in detail the components in a whole language classroom. The components were developed so that teachers would be able to better understand the practice of whole language and provide a framework for that practice.

There are a few things one needs to keep in mind as we describe these components. It is impossible for a teacher to provide time for all the components each day as described below. There is not enough time in a school day to provide experiences in each of the components and also teach other content subjects. Therefore, while the components will be described in detail and presented with a structured guideline in this chapter for the teacher's understanding, it would be best to refer to Chapter 16 to understand how the components work together in a classroom. The structured guidelines of the components are useful in getting started but are meant to be flexible. Suggested activities for each component are also included but are not exhaustive.

Moreover, during the experience of each component, the teacher will want to integrate listening, speaking, reading, and writing because we know that these language arts are influenced by each other and develop best in an integrated setting. Some components will emphasize one language art over others but the teacher will need to try and integrate them all. Furthermore, for each purpose the teacher has for providing a specific experience in a component, the experience will need to include the four aspects of language learning: model/demonstration, interaction, support, and independence.

For example, if a teacher wants to give her children experience with tall tales in the Shared Reading component, then s/he will want to have the children read a tall tale as the model, and interact with the concept of tall tale by discussing the characteristics. During the discussion the teacher will support the children's learning by using probing questions and showing examples of the characteristics. Lastly, the teacher will want to have the children independently recognize some characteristics of tall tales. This independent activity is part of the follow-up activity of Shared Reading.

Read To

The first component we will be describing is Read To. In this component the teacher is modeling the reading act for the children. The model/demonstration aspect of language learning is emphasized as well as the listening and speaking aspects of the language arts. The teacher will want to try and select books that reflect other areas of study in her/his classroom such as a thematic unit or science unit. Discussing parts of the Read To book are helpful in developing oral expression.

Purposes: The purposes for reading aloud to children include:

- enjoyment and appreciation of literature
- demonstration of oral expression and interpretation of literature
- development of listening skills
- language development
- motivation and interest in the world of books
- introduction of theme, genre, style, specific language structures, author, or illustrator
- as a model of the role of reader

Organization of Class and Material Selection

Generally, Read To is presented to the whole class. The teacher usually has them gathered in a relaxed setting such as on the rug in a group.
The teacher selects books according to his/her purpose. The books are generally

above grade level in reading ability for the class and are, therefore, books the children probably would not read on their own.

Important Aspects of Read To

1. Select a book that is appropriate to be read aloud. Not all books can or should be read aloud. An appropriate read aloud book is captivating, interesting, and able to keep the attention of the students.

2. Children should be allowed to select books for reading aloud as well the teacher in order to develop ownership in class activities. Oftentimes, they select books to be read which follow the theme, topic, etc. being studied in class.

3. Time established for this activity will be dependent on the book and listening ability of the group. However, generally the primary grade (K-3) teachers read aloud to children for longer periods than the intermediate grade (4-6) teachers because Read To serves as a model for taking on the role of the reader which is developing in the primary grades. Intermediate grade children are capable of that role and are now developing independent reading skills. Moreover, Read To is important at all levels and time should be allocated for it every day.

Suggested Activities

1. Try changing voices for the characters in the story.

2. Play music to accent the book being read. For example: scary music for a Halloween story.

3. Dress-up as the storyteller of the book if it's appropriate for your book or as one of the characters.

4. Play a recording of a professional reading of the book for the children.

Shared Reading/Language Experience

Shared reading and language experience are usually given priority time in a classroom day because all of the language arts — listening, speaking, reading, and writing, and all of the language learning aspects of model/demonstrate, interaction, support, and independence, are present in this experience. These experiences usually develop the thematic unit or content subject. The teacher usually sets aside time each day for this important component. However, a teacher would not do both shared reading and language experience necessarily in one day.

Shared Reading

<u>Purposes:</u> The major purpose for Shared Reading is the opportunity to have the whole class read together a piece of literature and share in its understanding. Shared Reading is a time for general class discussion, instruction, and responding. The teacher selects the shared book to introduce, instruct, and discuss:

- genre
- theme
- content area
- conventions of print
- literary elements
- comprehension
- author style
- illustrator style
- vocabulary
- cueing strategies

Organization of Class and Material Selection

Generally, the whole class gets together on a rug in front of the teacher. The teacher selects the book to be shared based on his/her purpose for the shared reading. If the purpose includes specific reading instruction then each child will need to see the text. The teacher can use a big book, overhead transparency, or a class set of the text so each student has a copy. The teacher selects material that is at the average literacy level of her/his students. By aiming for the average literacy level of your class, most of the children will benefit from the Shared Reading experience. For the students whose literacy level is much below the level of the shared book, they will be experiencing a read to situation and develop their listening skills and background knowledge. These lower students will also feel a part of the whole class by their participation. A different type of follow-up activity may need to be provided for these students. The Literacy Level Chart in Chapter 9 gives approximate levels appropriate for specific grade levels but the teacher will need to determine the appropriate book based on his/her purpose as well as general ability of her class.

Important Aspects of Shared Reading

1. The shared book is to be read together with the teacher as leader. Then, the book is reread with the children becoming the leaders. The teacher provides the support necessary for the class to effectively read the text.

2. The teacher utilizes this opportunity to introduce, instruct, or discuss a major strategy and/or concept to the whole class.

3. The teacher and class respond to the shared reading in some form of a follow-up activity.

4. The children use the shared books for rereading on their own or to others.

Suggested Activities

1. If the teacher is introducing an author's style, genre, or an illustrator's style, the children can make their own class book as a rewriting of the shared book. For a rewrite in an author style or a specific genre, the teacher and the class discuss the shared book to establish the characteristics of the style or genre. The teacher then leads the rewriting by asking for topic suggestions. As a class, the new topic, setting, and characters are cooperatively developed into a rewriting of the shared book.

After the group story is rewritten, each child or group of children gets a larger sheet of paper with a sentence or two written on it from the group story. They draw a picture to match the sentence(s). After all the children are finished, the story is put back together in the appropriate sequence and a new book is available for reading.

In the case of an illustrator rewrite, the teacher and children write their own story and construct pictures for the story in the illustrator's style. The pictures might be photographs, paintings, or cutup tissue paper depending on the style.

2. The children with the assistance of the teacher can create a play or puppet show of the shared book. Parents and other students can be invited for the presentation. This play production involves various aspects of drama and provides an effective means to increase the students' knowledge base of drama.

3. The children can each create their own individual book following the style of the shared book. These books can be put on the computer for publishing purposes. The new books will serve as more books for others to read.

4. Children can create mobiles of story characters, story events, or other stories written or illustrated by the author/illustrator.

5. Children can write in diary form as if they were a character in the book. They could have different events happen to the character other than those in the book.

The children would need to respond to these other events as they think the character might.

6. The children could create a model scene of a favorite part or character in the book. Each child could share this with the class in an oral presentation.

7. The children could write a letter to a character in the book. The teacher would respond as that character back to the children.

8. A class letter or student letters can be written to the author of the shared book. Authors often respond to the children about their work.

Language Experience (Preschool - Grade 1)

Purposes: The primary purpose of Language Experience is to help the child see the connection between speech and print. It also has served as a model for writing stories.

Organization of Class and Material Selection

This activity takes place generally with the whole class in preschool, kindergarten, or first grade but can be done individually or in small group. In second and third grade it is done infrequently and only when the children need the awareness of speech and print. Paper and pen for the teacher to write the story are the necessary materials.

Important Aspects of Language Experience

1. The teacher writes down the child's story. The teacher is careful to use appropriate grammar, spelling, and punctuation because the child will be using it for

reading. If the child speaks using an inappropriate sentence, the teacher can simply restate it correctly. For example: The child says: "He goed for a walk." The teacher can reply: "Are you saying that 'He went for a walk' ?" The child usually agrees and the teacher writes down the appropriate sentence. The teacher can refer to the corrected structure as "book language." It is important to be cautious about lowering self-esteem and taking away ownership with the corrections of inappropriate language structures.

2. Language experience is particularly important to children at the pre-emergent level of literacy. For the other primary children, it can be useful two or three times a week. Once children are reading independently, its value diminishes.

3. The teacher-written story is used for shared reading material. The same purposes can be established for the story depending on the text written. If individual or small group stories are written, they can be useful in guided reading for that child or group.

Suggested Activities

The generally accepted procedure for Language Experience includes:

1. Teacher and children discuss what topic to write about. They brainstorm ideas and discuss an outline of what the story will contain.

2. The teacher asks the children to begin the story by giving the first sentence. The children are guided by the teacher as they write the story. The teacher refers to various aspects as s/he writes. The teacher might show the children how the middle needs to have the details of the story expanded and so on.

3. After the story is written, the children practice reading the story together as in Shared Reading. The teacher will also discuss the story for other purposes.

For some children, a language experience story might be a sentence in length. The teacher will need to assess her/his students' ability.

Guided Reading

"Guided reading is an approach which enables a teacher and a group of children to talk, read, and think their way purposefully through a text, making possible an early introduction to reading silently," states *Reading in Junior Classes* (1985, p.69). This statement about guided reading and its role in teaching children to read indicates the importance of this activity in developing literacy. Through guided reading, teachers pursue the basics of reading process instruction including strategies, skills, and vocabulary development.

The guided reading experience is the principle direct instructional component of the whole language approach at the primary level. In this setting, teachers assume a supporting role as children take on the role of the reader and writer. The support and interaction aspects of literacy learning are emphasized in this component, but model/demonstration and independence are also present.

Children need sufficient exposure to guided reading opportunities at each literacy level if they are to progress confidently to the next literacy level. Some children require many more opportunities to be supported in their efforts before internalizing the essential knowledge and strategies of the literacy level. Once they move on in the guided sequence of levels, earlier level books are read independently to reinforce competencies and build attitudes.

<u>Purposes:</u> The purposes for guided reading include:

- developing reading and writing strategies
- expanding thematic unit at student's literacy level
- author/illustrator exploration
- genre study
- literary elements development
- reinforcement and practice with literacy level
  behaviors

Organization of Class and Material Selection

To begin guided reading, it is necessary for the teacher to plan about a 40 minute time block for guided reading per day. During this time the classroom teacher will work with two groups of students for about 15 to 20 minutes per group. Generally, each group meets with the teacher 3-5 times per week. The frequency of meeting is up to teacher judgement. If the remedial reading teacher comes into the classroom to provide services, she can work with one or two guided groups as well. Students not working in a guided group with the teacher are working on shared reading follow-up activities, independent reading, project work, learning centers, or independent writing.

The teacher assesses her/his students for the appropriate literacy level (See Chapter 14). Following assessment for appropriate individual placement within a guided reading group, the teacher selects a book at that literacy level. Chapter 15 can assist the teacher in making the determination of appropriate literacy level for a book.

Since many books at various literacy levels are required by each teacher during a school year, we have found it helpful to establish a school bookroom filled with books of all the literacy levels. These books are color-labeled on the outside as to the specific literacy level. This color labeling makes it easy to select the books and replace them. The teachers in the school share these books for their guided reading groups.

Important Aspects of Guided Reading

1. The teacher selects from the appropriate literacy level behavior lists (see Chapters 10-12) two or three behaviors to target using the selected book. The teacher will need to read the book ahead to determine which behaviors might be best illustrated through that book. Suggested activities are provided in these chapters.

2. Since each literacy level has different challenges to be encountered, there is a specific General Instructional Format for Reading at each literacy level (see Chapters 10-12). These guidelines assist teachers in understanding when an appropriate methodology shift is recommended.

3. As the students demonstrate behaviors of that literacy level, the teacher assesses the students' progress with the benchmarks for that literacy level. More challenging books are presented to the students as they progress.

4. The teacher also provides a writing experience as an activity for the selected book. The children complete the activity with support from the teacher. This writing task supports the development of literacy behaviors targeted through use of this book.

Suggested Activities

For this component the suggested activities will be specific to the literacy level of the students. These activities can be found in Chapters 10-12. If the guided reading component is focusing on a different purpose, then those activities are developed with that purpose in mind.

Independent Reading

The independent reading component's goal is independence in reading. The teacher will want to focus on how children select independent reading books, responding to reading books, and sharing of reading books. Conferencing with students during this independent time provides for teacher support in independent reading. The mini lessons (see Glossary) demonstrate the behavior or strategies important to reading. The responding and sharing provide the opportunity for interaction with books and others.

Young children need procedures and practice with routines in order for this component to run smoothly. It is suggested that the aspects of this component be worked on slowly and mastered one at a time in order to be successful in using this component.

Purposes: The purposes for independent reading include:

- self selection of reading books
- silent reading
- responding to literature
- sharing of reading interests

Organization of Class and Material Selection

The organization of this component needs to be well planned in order for it to succeed. The teacher needs to establish the guidelines for this experience. For primary age children, it is suggested that independent reading time begin with short periods of time and then increase. It is also suggested that the teacher discuss and practice with the children each part of this component before expecting the children to be able to function independently.

Kindergarten and first grade children have difficulty selecting books they can read on their own. They often read the pictures of books rather than engaging with the text. It is helpful for these children to have book boxes. That is, the teacher selects several books according to the literacy levels the students have accomplished and places them in book boxes designated for those students. Then for independent reading time, the children select from their book box a book to read. In this way, the teacher can be assured that the children can actually read the text and will be able to respond to the text. Children do not always have to select from these book boxes but they are available. In second grade, the teachers can begin with book boxes and then gradually instruct the children how to select appropriate books from several sources including the school library. Until second grade, the children seem to have difficulty with the selection of books.

Independent reading includes a mini lesson to instruct children on a strategy of independent reading, silent reading time, responding to the literature read, conferencing with students, and sharing the independent books with the class. Teachers often have children keep folders for Independent Reading. In these folders the children can list the title, author, and when they completed the book. This listing can help teachers guide children in their selection and keep a record of books read. The folders can also be used to list conference discussions with the teacher.

Mini lessons at the introduction of this component usually take the form of procedural, that is, how the children participate in this component. Later on, the mini lessons include selection of books, exposure to different genre or topics, content of responses, and sharing techniques.

Silent reading time varies from 10 to 40 minutes of time. At the primary grades, the average time is about 15-20 minutes. The teacher needs to make this judgement according to the capability of the class. The teacher also reads silently during part of this time. The other time is spent with conferencing with students.

Conferencing with students requires record keeping and organization. The children will need to rotate their conference time so that the teacher can meet with all children in her/his class on a weekly basis if possible. The record keeping needs to be developed so that the teacher will know what was discussed last week and where do we want to go this week. This part of the Independent Reading component is most conducive to the intermediate grades 3-6 when independent reading time is longer. Teachers can also arrange for peer conferencing or can conference by walking around to individual students for a brief period of time.

Responding to literature can be oral, written, or in the form of projects. Teachers can group children together and ask for oral responses on their specific book. A journal can be established for responding to books. At the primary grade levels these written responses need a written framework or the children will continue to just say they like the book.

Some teachers begin written response by having the children first draw a picture of their favorite part. Then several times later they ask the children to write about their favorite part of the book. Next, they ask the children to write why it was their favorite part. They also ask the children to write how they felt about the book. This type of structure enhances the understanding of the children that responding to literature means discussing what aspects of the story meant something to you personally and what you learned from this experience. This type of written response is not typical for primary grade children but the framework assists in this goal.

Sharing books that have been read is usually a favorite of elementary children. In the primary grades the children usually tell why they liked the book and what others might find interesting in the book. The goal in sharing is to point out and discuss the characteristics of the author style as well as your own opinion about the book with support from the text. This goal is generally not reached until the intermediate grades.

Most primary age children have difficulty remaining engaged in all of these parts for the time it takes to experience them. Therefore, primary teachers usually focus on silent reading, oral responding, and some sharing of books. In second grade, the children are able to add responding by writing to the component. In third grade, the mini lessons and conferencing are included because the independent reading time can be successfully increased for much longer periods of time (approximately 30 minutes).

Important Aspects of Independent Reading

1. Independent reading has several parts but primary age children are not necessarily capable or mature enough to function successfully in them all. Moreover, since the emphasis of this component is on independence, the children move into independence with reading as they acquire the behaviors and strategies of the literacy levels.

2. Children should experience their own time with books on a daily basis. It does not have to be a formal independent reading time but the teacher should allow some time for this independent reading.

3. Planning and organization are a must for this component in the classroom if it is to be successful. Record keeping is also important to log the progress of one's students.

Suggested Activities

1. For students beginning to write written responses to literature, developing a journal with title, author, and a response question may be useful. This structure will help to focus the young children as they respond and also provide a booklet for the teacher to observe the student's progress.

2. Set-up a special sharing time for books when the class invites their parents, the principal, reading teacher, etc. to attend. This activity will increase the parental awareness of whole language and also help them to feel a part of the process. The children can read their favorite part and then tell why it is their favorite part.

3. Projects are motivating in responding to the books the students are reading. Children can draw scenes from their books depicting the sequence of the story. They can make three-dimensional figures of scenes from their books.

Character mobiles are also interesting. The children draws one character and then several key parts which describe the attributes of the character. These can be displayed in the form of a mobile.

4. A class newspaper can be developed. In this newspaper, the children report on their independent reading books. They can either write their own articles or report on a classmate's book. Sharing this newspaper with other classrooms and

the parents will be helpful in demonstrating the wide variety of reading material children can read when given the opportunity to read independently.

Guided Writing

Guided writing is an important component in that it demonstrates to the developing writer some significant strategies useful to improve one's writing skills. The teacher's role is one of supporting or guiding the child through this writing process. This component provides for the children the opportunity to try different styles and forms of writing. The children interact with their writing and are given guidance by the teacher to develop these different styles and forms.

Purposes: The purposes for Guided Writing include:

- demonstration of specific genres
- demonstration of authors/illustrators
- developing the mechanics of writing
- experiencing a variety of writing forms/styles
- taking on the role of author
- revising writing pieces

Organization of Class and Material Selection

The teacher will need to establish a writing center or section with supplies for writing like pencils, erasers, different types of paper, stapler, clips, scissors, dictionary, etc. The children can utilize this center for all of their writing needs.

At the elementary and especially the primary level, we have found individual dictionaries to be useful. These dictionaries can be made of paper or commercially prepared. In each of the dictionaries are some common words the children will want to know how to spell. There will also be several spaces for additional words to be written. When a child doesn't know how to spell a word and wants to use it, then s/he approaches the teacher with her/his dictionary in hand. The teacher writes this word in the dictionary. Now, the child can use it in his/her writing and then reuse it at another time. This dictionary provides the opportunity for children to learn the uses of dictionaries.

Most often in this component, the whole class will work on a writing project. For example, in the Shared Reading component the class is reading about fairy tales. In the Guided Writing component, the project might be to write a fairy tale of their own. The teacher would discuss and develop the characteristics of a fairy tale through demonstration, i.e. s/he would read several fairy tales to the children and highlight the characteristics. Then, the teacher would guide the children through their own writing of a fairy tale. This project would take several weeks.

The teacher would plan for instructional sessions for each Guided Writing experience. These instructional sessions would guide the children through the steps of writing a fairy tale. Some sessions would involve content and others would involve mechanics. During a Guided Writing project, the children would follow the steps of the writing process: prewriting, drafting, revising, editing, and publishing. Prewriting is the preparation step before actual composing. The children are brainstorming topics, deciding on the purpose of the writing and the audience for the writing. Drafting is the writing of the piece without regard for mechanics or spelling. It's putting your ideas down on paper. Revising is assessing the draft and rewriting subsequent drafts in order to be clear on the message. Editing is reading the revised piece for grammatical, punctuation, capitalization, and spelling errors. Style and form are also considerations in editing. Lastly, the writing piece may be published by hanging it on a bulletin board, making it into a book, or having it typed on the computer. Sharing it before the class is another form of publishing. The instructional sessions might also focus on one of these steps.

Sometimes Guided Writing is not a project but a brief writing piece that the teacher determines that her/his class requires for further study. For example, the Guided Writing activity for one day might be a follow-up to the Shared Reading. In this case, the teacher might guide the children through how to write a description of a character in an alternate setting. The Guided Writing component is most important for its supporting and guiding aspects in the development of a writer.

Important Aspects of Guided Writing

1. Guided Writing is an important component for assisting children in the development of writing ability. The teacher can plan an extensive project or can plan shorter writing experiences. The goal of Guided Writing is to encourage writing development and a broadening of scope of writing strategies.

2. Guided Writing experiences follow the writing process steps of prewriting, drafting, revising, editing, and publishing. At the kindergarten and first grade levels, revising and editing are not usually a major focus. Young children usually feel that once they've written something, it's done. These concepts of revising and editing are more successful beginning in grade 2.

3. The teacher's role in Guided Writing is one of support and guidance.

4. Guided Writing projects can take several weeks to complete.

5. The teacher determines the needs of her class in the area of writing. From these needs, s/he plans for the Guided Writing experiences which will meet these needs.

6. Most elementary teachers find that they need to limit the number of Guided Writing projects due to the length. However, they continue to use Guided Writing on a daily basis in the form of the shorter aspects integrated in the other components or for brief instructional sessions.

Suggested Activities

1. Select Guided Writing projects that relate to the thematic units you plan to use during the school year.

2. Children seem to respond positively to writing forms that they have had experience with in other components. Therefore, select writing forms the children have had exposure to in Read To, Shared Reading, or Guided Reading.

3. Involve the special area teachers (art, music, etc.) in your Guided Writing projects. For example, the art teacher can assist in the illustrations by presenting the children with different art forms for the drawings.

4. As a culminating activity for the Guided Writing projects, invite your parents and other school personnel to attend a formal presentation and sharing of these projects.

5. One Guided Writing project could be writing letters. The children could establish pen pals in another state or country and write to them.

6. Older children could write stories about or for younger children. These stories would be presented on a special day when the classes meet to share their work. The teacher could use any genre for this writing or the stories could be rewrites of a literature piece.

Independent Writing

Independent Writing is similar to Independent Reading in format and intent. This component emphasizes independence in writing, an important goal in language arts instruction. The student interacts with the writing and is supported somewhat by the teacher in conferencing. The students are encouraged in this component to individually select topics for writing and utilize their writing skills independently.

<u>Purposes:</u> The purposes for Independent Writing include:

- develop individual style and interests in writing
- develop strategies that promote independence in writing
- the ability to assess one's own needs in writing and seek assistance in these areas

Organization of Class and Material Selection

Independent Writing is similar to Guided Writing in that a writing center or section is useful, as well as a writing dictionary for each student. The parts of this component are similar to Independent Reading and include mini lesson, writing, conferencing, and sharing of writing. As in Independent Reading, all of the component parts of Independent Writing are difficult to handle for young children due to maturity and the amount of time required for this experience. Therefore, the parts of Independent Writing focused on in the primary grades usually include writing time on self-selected topics and sharing of writing.

The mini lesson in Independent Writing is selected by the teacher who determines the writing needs of her/his class. At the initial implementation of this component, the mini lessons will focus on procedural aspects such as topic selection or revising techniques. As the component is established, the mini lessons will become mostly content such as writing a good lead for a story.

The writing time in Independent Writing focuses on self-selected topics. The children have complete ownership over their writing in this component. The teacher's role is one of facilitator in encouraging writing independently. In the primary grades the time for writing varies but young children can usually engage in it for about 20 minutes. At the intermediate grades, the average time is usually 40 minutes.

Conferencing for Independent Writing involves organization and record keeping as in Independent Reading. The children will need to rotate their conference time so that the teacher can meet with all children in her/his class on a weekly basis. The record keeping needs to be developed so that the teacher will know the status of each student and the direction in which to proceed. This part of the Independent Writing component is most conducive to the intermediate grades 3-6 when Independent Writing time is longer. Teachers can also arrange for other types of conferencing such as peer conferencing or conferencing by walking around to students.

Sharing of writing pieces becomes very special in Independent Writing. The children have written pieces that are very close to them. It is important that the teacher establish guidelines for this time. Many children's self-esteem is fragile in this setting. This time needs to be established as a nurturing time. Trust is an important ingredient for the class to feel at ease in sharing their work.

During the Independent Writing experience, as in Guided Writing, the children would follow the steps of the writing process: prewriting, drafting, revising, editing, and publishing. (See Guided Writing component for details.)

Teachers often have students keep a writing folder with their work in progress. These folders can be filed in the writing center or some other location. In the writing folder, the teacher can list the conference discussions and student goals for writing. This folder seems to be helpful in classroom management of this component.

Important Aspects of Independent Writing

1. Independent Writing is an important component in developing life-long writers. All parts of the component may not be appropriate for all ages, but all ages need writing time on a daily basis.

2. Since Independent Writing involves self-selected topics, the teacher should be aware that the sharing of these pieces may be very emotional for the child. Therefore, sharing time needs to have guidelines that nurture children in writing.

3. Independent Writing uses the writing process steps of prewriting, drafting, revising, editing, and publishing. However, in kindergarten and grade 1 revising and editing are not a focus. Children at grade 2 are better able to understand the

concepts of revising and editing.

4. Children may remain on one topic for several weeks or months. It depends on their interest and knowledge. Teachers can encourage completion but it is not unusual to have students remaining with a topic for several weeks.

Suggested Activities

1. During sharing time have the students write a positive comment on an index card and give it to the writer. These positive comments develop trust and mutual respect among class members.

2. To assist students in the writing process steps, have charts made of the various steps. Listed on these charts would be questions the children need to ask themselves as they go through the process such as "Did I spell all my words correctly?" These charts could then be displayed in the classroom.

3. The two areas that seem to give students difficulty are revising and editing. As a class, develop checklists for revising and editing to act as reminders as the students write. These checklists could become part of their writing folders.

4. The class can establish a publishing center of works completed by the students. This center can make the writing pieces of the students available to all for enjoyment and appreciation.

5. Writing pieces written by the students can be put into book form and sent to the school library for use. Other students in the school can sign out these books and share in the writing.

Summary

1. Reading, writing, listening, and speaking are integrated throughout the whole language components. Some components focus on one area more than others. The teacher's goal is to include them all to some extent in each component.

2. The learning aspects of model/demonstration, interaction, support, and independence are important to all components. Some components lend themselves more readily to a certain aspect than others. In order to promote learning, all aspects need to be present to some degree.

3. This chapter describes each component in detail giving the teacher guidelines in instruction, activities, and framework. Listed below is a quick reference form on each component for teachers.

Outline of Whole Language Components

Read To

Teacher reads story for enjoyment, appreciation
Teacher discusses story with class

Shared Reading

Teacher introduces story and links prior knowledge
Teacher and children read story together orally or silently
Teacher instructs in strategies for word study and
understanding the text
Teacher presents follow-up activity which reinforces/expands
strategy instruction

Guided Reading

Teacher introduces purpose for reading
Student reads text with teacher support
Teacher instructs in literacy level strategies
Teacher presents follow-up reinforcement on strategies

Independent Reading

Teacher instructs mini lesson
Teacher and class read silently
Teacher conferences with students
Students respond to books
Class shares books

Guided Writing

Teacher demonstrates strategies (content, grammar, editing, genre)
Teacher assists students as they write
Teacher conferences with students to reinforce strategies
Class shares writing

Independent Writing

Teacher instructs mini lesson
Teacher and class write silently
Teacher conferences with students
Class shares writing

Chapter 7   Whole Language in the Preschool and Kindergarten

Preschool and/or kindergarten are the first opportunities some children have with literacy experiences. Moreover, other children come to school with a background in literacy already developed. Almost all children come to school with a speaking language. Let's explore these aspects more closely.

A speaking language or oral language develops from birth and influences literacy development or reading and writing. In order for a child to be able to understand and develop the two-dimensional world of print, s/he needs to have basic understandings about language and feel secure with his/her speaking language. Here is a diagram explaining the relationship between reading, writing, listening, and speaking.

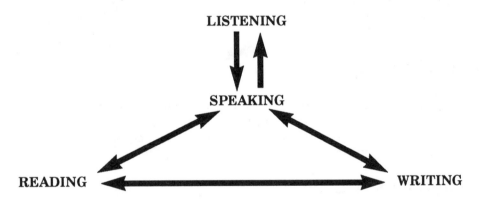

As this diagram indicates speaking and listening directly influence each other and encourage each other. The oral language or speaking has an impact on both reading and writing, but reading and writing also influence each other. These relationships are important to understand for the preschool or kindergarten teacher as s/he plans for literacy experiences in her/his classroom.

Most teachers will agree that children who come to school reading and/or writing usually come from homes where many literacy experiences have taken place. These parents often tell the teacher that they aren't sure how the child learned to read or write but it just happened. Understanding the kinds of literacy experiences these children encountered will be helpful in designing the preschool and kindergarten curriculum.

In most literate home environments, reading to the children is a priority. These children are read to on a daily basis, usually several times a day. Parents, themselves, read openly in front of the children and the home has many different kinds of reading materials available (books, newspapers, magazines, etc.). There are usually several different bookcases in the house with different types of books. A special time is devoted to reading for the children as well as the adults.

The interactions in all forms — oral, print, and written — with children and adults are significant. Parents interacting with the child in conversation will play a supportive role, that is, they will guide the child in communicating his/her message. For example, if the child said "cookie" the parent might respond, "Do you want a cookie?" or "These are frosted cookies." The child would respond and the interaction would continue until the message was communicated. In reading to the child, these parents involve the child in the sharing of the book. They have the child repeat the funny phrases or make the sounds of the animals. The parents enjoy the book together with the child and converse over its contents. The child asks for his/her favorite books to be read over and over again. The parents accommodate.

In the writing interactions, the parents often provide coloring books, clay, paper, crayons, etc. so the child has experiences with writing. Magnetic letters are often on the refrigerator for the child to recognize and play with among other toys. The parent may write the child's name or make it out of magnetic letters. The parent may draw pictures with the child, explaining the drawing to the child in a story format. Everyday activities like going shopping become learning opportunities. The parents answer the numerous questions of the child and will often point out items or pictures of things the child is familiar with from home like apples or elephant pictures. Even the toys played with in the home encourage interactions that expand the child's development. The parents often buy thematic toy items like the zoo and all the animals or the train set with the village. These interactions encourage children to build concepts and knowledge about their world.

In the school setting the teacher will want to plan for the same types of experiences and also encourage more literacy development. Let's look at four areas of development: social-attitudinal, sounds of the language, written language, and thematic play. As we examine these aspects we will keep in mind the learning factors of model/demonstration, interaction, support, and independence.

Social/Attitudinal

In this area of social/attitudinal, the teacher strives to plan literacy experiences which promote social interaction and a positive attitude toward learning. Children naturally want to use their language with peers and the teacher. However, the goal of the teacher is to promote growth in this area. To do this the teacher will want to structure activities. For example, most children at this age want to share a story from home, or show and tell. This activity is helpful in oral presentation skills for the children but can also be helpful to the class in other ways. As each child speaks, the teacher can list on chart paper the topic the child spoke about to the class. After the teacher has modeled several topics, s/he can have the class decide on the topic that the child spoke (summary of a story). This connection to written language can enhance children's awareness of print. Another activity from show and tell can be to select one child's story and write a language experience story about it. This story can be reread by the children and become part of a class book of stories. Each time the teacher can select a different child until the book has a story from each child in the class.

A different kind of interaction to be encouraged is between children. A cooperative activity can be planned in which this type of interaction is structured. An example would be that the teacher develop a painting activity in which two children paint one picture to tell a story. The paired children would need to discuss what story is to be told or what picture is to be drawn. Each item would need to be decided and cooperatively planned. This particular activity would require guidance from the teacher as to the guidelines for cooperative work, an important life skill. The importance of this interaction is that it promotes development in oral communication. The children will need to refine their speaking language or use different language to ensure that they are understood and are able to cooperatively complete the painting.

Throughout all learning experiences the teacher will want to encourage:
-children to be risk-takers by understanding that they can succeed
  or fail and be accepted

-children to communicate their intent to others but respect other
  people's perspectives

-learning activities that are guided by the teacher but allow for
  independent learning of the children

-a variety of activities that have relevance to the children in order
  to expand their knowledge base

From these type of experiences the children will be encouraged to develop communication skills, different strategies for interaction (cooperative, oral presentation, etc.), respect for other children's learning as well as their own, and an enhancement of self-esteem.

Sounds of the Language

In this area the teacher is concerned about promoting facility with the language and an awareness of the components of language: meaning, structure, words, syllables, and sounds. A priority in promoting literacy development is an understanding of how the language works and how the student can develop the ability to use language to communicate with his/her world as well as understand other people's use of the language, speaking or written.

Many traditional activities at the preschool and kindergarten level continue to support and encourage this area. Some of these activities include finger plays, moving to the rhythm of the song, movement songs or acting out the song, learning letters and their sounds, clapping and tapping out patterns of sound with musical instruments, round singing, tongue twisters, and choral repetitions of poems or stories. In the traditional approach, these activities would often be done in isolation or not related to other activities but as separate units. In whole language these activities become integrated into the theme or an area of study like the farm or growing flowers. This integration requires that the whole language teacher become knowledgeable of many activities and skillful in planning them into the overall theme or unit.

Other activities which can be developed in this area are rewrites, language segmenting, and labeling of objects. Rewrites are stories that copy different styles or forms of literature. The story elements are changed to fit a different situation. For example: Using the nursery rhyme of Jack and Jill, the teacher rewrites the rhyme using names of two children in her/his class.

Language segmenting activities can include the tapping out of sentences into words, one tap per word, or clapping out the syllables in multi-syllable words given by the teacher. Other activities include giving a word to the children such as bike, asking them to change the word by putting in a "l" sound for "b," and having them tell the new word. Blocks can be used as markers for each sound the children hear in a one-syllable familiar word like hot. These language segmenting activities will foster the awareness of the components of the language, thereby assisting in the transition from oral to written language.

Labeling objects may seem to be a simple activity but is also very useful in promoting literacy. The teacher and children can cooperatively label objects and discuss the differences in words that they might use to label the same object. The children can be asked to categorize these word labels by category (furniture) or by sound, either initial letters the same or words that rhyme. This develops word awareness.

In summary, these experiences and activities will acquaint children with the language, develop facility, and help them to become aware of the uses and components of language.

Written Language

Encouraging writing experiences of all kinds throughout the activities of the day is essential to literacy development. Many activities involving writing have already been discussed in the previous two areas. A few more will be discussed here.

Language experience both individually with a student and with a whole class should be a priority in a weekly schedule. Even though this process (See

Chapter 6 for the step-by-step process) can be lengthy, it is well worth the effort. From this one experience the children can learn about story development, word awareness, sound awareness, vocabulary development, and language structure. These stories can be illustrated by the children and displayed.

Sharing a story with the class through Read To or Shared Reading activities is very helpful at this level (See Chapter 6). Reading books, poems, etc. to children helps to model the written language to the children. Book language is often not the same as speaking language. Shared reading at this level works best with big books, either commercial or teacher prepared. This format allows the teacher to show print to her/his whole class and to demonstrate what reading looks like. The teacher and class can discuss the author's message and make predictions in the story. The teacher at this level will point out various conventions of print, vocabulary words, and language structure. The follow-up activity may be a drawing of their favorite part. The teacher's intent is an awareness of books and their language.

Each classroom should be equipped with a writing supply center. This center would have supplies for the children to try out writing. These supplies would provide the setting for experimentation and risk-taking.

Lastly, the teacher might want to plan an activity time where s/he specifically asks the children to write for her/him. For example, the class has just returned from the zoo. The teacher has asked each child to draw a picture of his/her favorite part. After the children have drawn their pictures, they are asked to write a couple of letters or words describing their picture. Depending on abilities this task may be overwhelming for some children. In these cases, they would not be asked to write. The teacher could write the word or words for them using the language experience technique.

Thematic Play

Morrow and Rand (1991) support the concept that play is an important element in promoting literacy. They feel that play can encourage literacy through classroom design. One area of classroom design emphasized is thematic play or designating a place in the classroom based on a theme. Morrow and Rand suggest various themes such as a veterinarian's office, restaurant, supermarket, post office, and airport. These theme areas reenact the real life situation. For example, in the restaurant there would be a menu, play money, a table, dishes, play food, signs with the name of the restaurant or other advertisements, etc. The children would play in this area and learn what the various written messages were, write down the menu orders, and play act the situation. The possibilities in play areas like these are endless.

In addition to the thematic play described by Morrow and Rand, other themes in play can be developed. These areas could include a library, science center, travel center, math center, and health center. While these areas would involve perhaps more activities rather than reenactment, the idea would be similar. The children would be involved in the world of science or in visiting a foreign land in which a child in the class might have his/her roots. In each of these areas the child would see labels of items, be able to manipulate objects, play games, etc.

The preparation of these thematic play areas would be time consuming but could serve as valuable, meaningful activities promoting literacy development. Research seems to support these types of early learning activities.

In conclusion, these four areas of social/attitudinal, sounds of the language, written language, and thematic play are important aspects in a preschool or kindergarten for literacy development. This is not to suggest that they are the only areas in a program. It also is important to understand that these areas are not separate but integrated. As you probably realized, in the thematic play, for example, written language, sounds of the language, and social/attitudinal were all integrated. In whole language, the practice reflects the learning theory that people learn through an integrated process.

An Example of a Thematic Unit

Teachers seem to relate best when specific examples are given to explain the concept. The following is an outline of a one-week unit on spring. There is also one day's plans during this week. The length of time for these sessions has not been given because each teacher will need to plan the time according to class ability.

General Theme

The general theme is spring. This teacher will focus on flowers, birds, insects, life cycle, and the concept of change. In the classroom are these centers: chicken eggs in an incubator with a life cycle poster of the chicken, a writing supply center, a library center with spring-theme books displayed, a paint center, an art center, a change center in which several objects relating to spring are displayed and changed each day, and an insect center with containers displaying insects and pictures of insects. The theme unit will begin with the introduction of one theme center per day. The writing, library, and art center are always present.

Study Format

The teacher has established her/his daily routine to include a Read To session, Shared Reading, and center activities. When possible volunteer parents assist in the center activities. Other routines are established such as calendar and weather charts, snack or lunch time, and show and tell. It is also important to note that these activities are based on a full-day session and would need to be reduced for half-day sessions.

One Day's Plans

Read To:
The Very Quiet Cricket by Eric Carle (New York: Philomel Books, 1990). This book was chosen because the subject matter is insects, the text is simple and short, the message has charm and value, the book is interesting and motivating, and the book has a cricket sound in it which chirps at the end to add a different dimension.

Shared Reading:
Pumpkin, Pumpkin by J. Titherington (New York: Scholastic, 1986). This book would be used in big book format. The story is about a boy and the growth of a pumpkin. It's a simple, beautiful story. The teacher would read the story to the children first and point to each word as s/he reads to help show children the separation of words in print. Throughout the reading the teacher would stop for

clarification of understanding and to predict the next part of the story. After the initial reading, the teacher would ask the children to join in the reading for a second time. Next, the teacher would distribute three or four word cards. The teacher and class would read a sentence from the book and ask the child with a word card to match her/his word on the card in the sentence. This activity may be too difficult for some children so the teacher will need to use her/his own judgement.

Other follow-up activities possible with this book are:

-have students draw three pictures, on separate sheets of paper, of the beginning, middle, and end of the story.

-give students a packet of word cards from one page in the story; the students match the word cards with the text of the story.

-give children a pumpkin drawn on a sheet of paper; ask them to decide what they would do with this grown pumpkin, ex: make a pumpkin pie, jack-o-lantern; they are to make the pumpkin into it or draw the face inside the pumpkin.

-have students draw their own story of what might have happened to the pumpkin; then the children are asked to write what is happening to their pumpkin; the teacher would need to assist most children in this activity by helping them hear the sounds in words and identifying the letter to represent the sound.

Centers:

There would be four centers open: library center, science center, art center, and change center. In the art center would be an activity that involved making spring flowers for display. The library center would have books on insects, flowers, and birds. The children would be asked to arrange the books under the appropriate written label (birds, flowers, or insects). They would select their favorite book and tell why it is their favorite.

The science center would have insects and the children would be asked to explore the science and draw their favorite insect and tell the class why it is their favorite. Lastly, the change center would have two more spring items (broken robin's egg, daffodil) than it did yesterday. The children would have to identify which items were added by selecting the picture-word cards that represent the items.

Language Experience:

At the conclusion of the center activities, the teacher would call the children together on the rug. S/he would ask the children who experienced the change center to describe the items added today. These descriptions would be listed on a chart. This chart would continue each day until all of the spring items were listed with descriptions.

Next, the teacher would ask the children who drew their favorite insect to come to the front of the class. They would show their picture and tell why it is their favorite. The teacher would write the name of the insect on their paper and perhaps a phrase or sentence telling why they liked it.

Other activities:

Writing activity - Each child is developing a spring book. The children draw pictures and write sentences to tell the story. Some children will not be able to write more than a letter or two, but encouraging them to try is important.

Movement activity - A short activity that develops coordination could be to have the children show how different insects move. Some suggested insect movements include butterfly, ant, and bee. Music could also be incorporated into this activity.

Nature walk - For physical activity and to develop observational skills, the class would take a nature walk to a nearby park or on the school grounds. The teacher would explain that they will be looking for insects, signs of spring, birds, and flowers. When they returned to the classroom, these observations would be discussed, written about, and illustrated.

Home activity - Parent involvement is essential to literacy development. Each day the teacher will want to include an activity which can be shared with parents. For this day, the children could take home a completed written story to read to their parents. The children could also be asked to have their parents guess which insect they are from their movements.

In conclusion, this example represents how a teacher might integrate the literacy experiences in a thematic unit and foster literacy growth.

Summary

1. Literacy experiences in the preschool and kindergarten need to include listening, speaking, reading, and writing because of the interdependence to these language arts.

2. Preschool and kindergarten activities to promote literacy should include: social/attitudinal, sounds of the language, written language, and thematic play areas.

3. A typical day in early learning in whole language would focus on the Read To and Shared Reading components and involve writing experiences.

Chapter 8   Selecting Literature for the Whole Language Classroom: Using the Librarian as a Resource

In every aspect of whole language teaching there is collaboration, and the selection of books is no exception. A skilled whole language teacher has a knowledge base of many different pieces of literature in many different genres. Even with this broad knowledge base, the skilled whole language teacher knows that using all resources, including people, to effectively teach is a must. This teacher also knows that this learning process never ends and that these resource people are a part of a teacher's network for teaching whole language. The librarian is an important resource to the teaching of whole language.

Role of Librarian

The librarian has knowledge and skills that a typical teacher does not possess. These knowledge and skills include an understanding of the depth and breath of literature, knowledge of most recently published books, knowledge of resources that can be helpful in literature study, and access to a network of other librarians and libraries which can provide the kinds of resources a whole language program requires. Therefore, one key aspect to the role of a librarian is as a resource provider to whole language teachers. When a teacher begins to use whole language teaching methods, s/he must select books and materials at a variety of levels for her/his students to use in the unit of study. In the traditional classroom, the textbooks were the main source of reading information for the unit of study. In whole language, the main source for the unit of study becomes the library.

Another aspect to the role of librarian is assisting children on a larger scale with independent book selection. Librarians have always been helpful to children as they selected books but now, in addition to interest areas, the librarian needs to understand the literacy levels for the primary children. Before whole language the primary children often took books out of the library for their parents to read. Now, in addition to selecting books for their parents to read, they want books they can read. In whole language the attitude that everyone is a reader is encouraged. The emergent and early reader will require carefully selected books if they are to be able to read the text. The librarian can be helpful in this selection if s/he has knowledge of the type of books necessary for the child's literacy level.

Lastly, the librarian can act as a facilitator of literature to expand the classroom teacher's knowledge and expand the children's knowledge of literature. Our teachers find that book talks by the librarian two or three times a school year are helpful in introducing the new books in the library. The librarian has knowledge of the curriculum content in all subject areas at each grade level and seeks to purchase books in these areas to assist the teachers. Furthermore, the library sessions the children attend in the library are structured around what is presently being taught in the classroom. For example, a second grade teacher may be studying fairy tales with her/his students. The library sessions for those weeks will include the reading and discussion of fairy tales that the classroom teacher would not have introduced or a further development of the classroom teacher's work. The classroom teacher may be discussing Sleeping Beauty stories and the librarian will read another version to the children and discuss it. This aspect of the role of a librarian serves to integrate the library with the whole language program.

Why the Selection of Books Is Important

In the traditional basal program the selection of reading material to teach reading was arranged in an anthology and utilized throughout the school year. The basal authors determined which skills would be taught with each reading selection. The teacher sometimes supplemented this anthology with other reading selections for other purposes.

In whole language there is a different point of view. First of all the teacher needs to assess the abilities of his/her students, and then the teacher selects a piece of literature for a specific purpose and literacy level of his/her students. For example, it would be difficult for first grade children to understand the author style of Lois Lowery in *Number the Stars* (Boston: Houghton Mifflin, 1989) due to the literacy level of first grade children, their experiential background, and inappropriate subject matter for first graders.

The teacher's purposes can include promoting reading development, studying an author style, learning information about something, or studying a genre. Whatever the purpose is, the teacher will either be supported by the reading material selected or be limited in the ability to support and challenge his/her students as they read.

Therefore, the books the teacher selects for her students' reading or makes available to the students for reading is a vital key in promoting literacy development in her/his students. Teachers must make careful, informed selections in reading materials and teach these selection abilities to their students.

Selecting Books for Read To, Shared Reading, Guided Reading, and Independent Reading

In order to carefully select books for each whole language component, the first priority is to look at the purpose the book will serve. If the purpose is to illustrate author style, then the literacy level of the book is not as important as a representative reading selection depicting the characteristics of the author's style. On the other hand, if the purpose is to assist children in learning how to read, then the literacy level is essential. Learning to read is promoted when reading material gives children some challenges in the text but not so overwhelming that the children experience frustration and struggle in reading the text. In conclusion, the purpose the book will serve is the driving force behind why the teacher selects that particular book.

The second aspect to look at is the whole language component (Read To, Shared Reading, etc.) it will serve in the literacy experience.

In **Read To**, the teacher generally selects books which are significantly above where most of his/her students are capable of reading at this time. The book should promote listening ability in terms of attentiveness and comprehension. Not every book can be read aloud to children and keep their attention. Not every book when read aloud is easily understood. Therefore, an important consideration factor is the purpose of **Read To**. At the early primary grade levels (Preschool, K, 1) books with rhythmical language, rhymes, or simple straightforward plots seem to work best. Picture books which have illustrations that enhance the text or explain the text are also useful. The amount of text and length should be gradually increased so that the children's ability to attend and remember can increase. In second grade and third grade longer picture books and chapter books work well in developing their language abilities.

In **Shared Reading** the teacher is focusing on print and having students actually experience the reading together. Therefore, each child should have a copy or be able to see the print such as in big books or by using an overhead transparency of the text. In addition, the teacher will want to select a book which can be read with support by many of the children in the class. The teacher's intent in **Shared Reading** is to have many children experience reading the text. If the literacy level is too difficult for the majority of students, then the intent of **Shared Reading** will be diminished.

In **Guided Reading** the student takes on the role of reader. Therefore, literacy level is crucial in this component. The student reads the text with the support of the teacher. The teacher will need to assess carefully the competencies of her/his students and then select books at their literacy level. **Guided Reading** is the "heart of the whole language program" as Andrea Butler indicates. (Butler, 1988, p. 3) Here are some specific guidelines for the selection of books for **Guided Reading**.

Choosing Guided Reading Books

Teachers find the selection of guided reading books to be difficult because publishers have been careless in designating levels or they are non-existent. In Chapter 15 a procedure for determining the literacy level of literature is discussed. However, below is a brief description of the characteristics of each level book. This description will assist the librarian for general classification if students need assistance and the classroom teacher for her/his classroom library. Please turn to Chapter 15 if a specific level for a book is needed.

Characteristics of Type of Books for Literacy Level

Emergent Books

Emergent books usually have only one sentence or line per page. This sentence matches what is seen in the picture. The basic stem of the sentence is repetitive on almost all pages. Ex: I like cars. I like toys. In order for the book to be of value in the emergent level it must have one-to-one text-picture match. The books at this level are often commentaries. That is, they are books centered around one topic with limited story line. The books are highly repetitive.

Early 1

The Early 1 books focus on continued picture-text match, repetition; and now the introduction of word differences begins. Children are required to use context and word differences to determine the unfamiliar words. These books generally have no more than two lines of print and have a basic text stem with changes at the end and/or beginning of the stem (i.e. Sally runs to school. Tom runs to the store.). A different opening and/or closing statement from the structure of the basic stem is predominant. While the books are often commentaries, story lines are becoming more frequent.

Early 2

The Early 2 books contain more print (about 2-3 lines of print), more word differences from basic text stem, and more than one basic text stem. They are still repetitive. The children require some sight vocabulary and the use of some sound/symbol to read and understand these books. The pictures continue to support the text but more is being said in the text than is seen in the picture.

Early 3

Early 3 books drop the basic text stem aspect of language structure and utilize simple sentence structures. The sentences are short and usually contain familiar or common vocabulary words. The students are required to have a building sight vocabulary and the application of sound/symbol to read these books. The pictures still support the text but the one-to-one match is gone. There is sometimes repetition of sections of the story rather than of individual sentences. A story line has emerged in these books but there is little depth or detail.

Early 4

Early 4 books have pictures that support the text but most of the meaning is derived from the text. The books have a definite story plot with some detail. The sentence structures are compound sentences and simple sentences. They are also varied in the development of the story. Context, sentence structure, and sound/symbol are all necessary cueing strategies that need to be in place for the students to read these books. This level has the children practicing those strategies in longer texts than Early 3.

Fluency 1

In Fluency 1 books with the cueing strategies in place, the text is much longer and usually there are chapters. The sentences are relatively simple but more details are in the text than in the pictures. The pictures are on the general theme and enhance the plot. Most of these books are written at the literal level of understanding.

Fluency 2

Fluency 2 books begin to introduce the children to the subtleties of the language. The text is written to encourage interpretation at a couple of areas. The text is longer per page and in chapters or the book is several pages in length. This requires the students to keep the story line in their memory over longer periods of time.

Fluency 3

In this level the text requires the students to use more frequent interpretation, perhaps on every page. The sentences are varied in complexity and style. Students expand their experiences with author style and genres.

Fluency 4

At this level the genres and author styles are a big focus. The students are capable of handling most text with minimal teacher support. Critical thinking skills, problem solving, and inferences are all major concerns for study in these books. The books are written with complex sentence structures and are lengthy.

Lastly, **Independent Reading** is when the student not only takes on the role of reader but also selects his/her own books for reading. The role of the teacher in this component is to have available the appropriate books of varying literacy levels, content, authors, etc. for selection. The teacher assists the students in learning how to select books on their own but the selection is the children's choice.

In conclusion, in order to select the appropriate book, the teacher will need to focus on his/her purpose for reading the book and the specific component to be used in the reading of the book. The difficulty the Skaneateles teachers experienced in the selection of books was in which books to select to promote reading development in any of the components. It appeared that after the students had learned to read, then the teacher was guided more by content and interest. However, in the primary years when reading is developing, giving a child a book they were interested in but were unable to successfully read was diminishing to the child's confidence in reading. Moreover, after the teachers were presented with the framework of the literacy levels discussed in Chapters 9-12, they were able to more appropriately select books and promote the reading development of their children. The books to be used in the program were leveled for the teachers. These leveled books provided the opportunities for children to demonstrate and practice literate behaviors.

Literary Form (Genre) Characteristics

Another area of importance in the selection of books is the literary form or genre. Many teachers starting out in whole language need guidelines as to what are the genres. The following chart is a brief description of the literary form and characteristics. This chart is only a guideline and includes the genres which primary teachers find work best with their students.

Genre	Characteristics
Fiction	
Folktales	This traditional literature has story lines that have recurring actions, one-dimensional characters, settings that are generic, and stories focusing on human problems and various cultures.
Fables	These stories, focus on animal characters depicting human problems and usually have a moral to teach.
Myths	These stories while often believed true from their culture, are often religious based and often explain natural phenomena.
Picture Books	The text can be repetitious or rhymical. The plots are often predictable and with simple story line. The illustrations often help to tell the story.

Fantasy	These stories depart from reality. The plots can involve heroes or heroines in unrealistic settings with unrealistic powers. They seem believable because the unreal is accepted as truth by the character and the story develops logically.
Science Fiction	Science fiction is similar to fantasy, but advanced scientific technology is depicted. The future of the human race is often the topic.
Realistic Fiction	The settings, characters, and plots of these books portray real life. The problems and predicaments are true to life.
Historical Fiction	These books, while fictitious, are set in history with appropriate historical facts of the time period.
Mystery	The plot is written with twists and turns in the resolution of a problem. Clues are written to keep the reader in suspense until the resolution.
Drama	The dialogue is the essence of the play. There are some statements about setting and characters but the story develops through dialogue.
Nonfiction	
Informational Books	These books are factual and will use description, narrative, or expository writing. They are logically organized with illustrations which enhance the information.
Biography	Biographies have people who have achieved something or are famous as their subjects.

	They use a narrative style with factual information about the person.
Books of True Experience	These books focus on an event or adventure in a person's life.
Letters, Journals, Diaries	This literature is adapted or based on original documents.
Newspapers/ News Magazines	These articles include a variety of information written in a direct style answering the basic questions who, what, when, where, why, how. Current events are the primary topics.

Poetry

Ballad	Ballads are similar to a song and tell the story of a hero or heroine.
Narrative	These poems tell a story with plot, characters, etc.
Lyric	These poems are rhymical with inspiring images.
Limerick	A limerick is usually humorous with a surprise ending. It is a five-line poem: first, second, fifth - rhyme; third, fourth-rhyme.
Haiku	Haiku involves poetry with nature as its primary topic. It has seventeen syllables, and three lines (5-7-5).
Cinquain	These poems have five lines with syllable patterns of 2-4-6-8-2 or 1-2-3-4-1.

| Concrete poems | The words and arrangement of words of the poem express the message of the poem. Ex: Dripping rain — poem has words arranged like raindrops. |

Summary

1. This chapter described the important role of the librarian as resource person and facilitator of literature in a whole language program.

2. The selection of literature is important in whole language because literature is the "textbook" of the program.

3. Several hints for book selection were described for each component and literacy level.

4. The different literary forms, genres, and brief descriptions were presented for whole language teachers as guidelines in the primary grades.

Chapter 9 Understanding the Literacy Levels: Developing a Framework for Learning to Read and Write

In teaching children to read and write using a whole language approach, certain attitudes and behaviors are encouraged to develop a lifelong reader and writer. These attitudes and behaviors for a reader include being a risk-taker and understanding that getting the author's message from the text is the ultimate goal. Readers understand that to get this message they must have facility with cueing strategies — to know when to use which at what time. They must know how to use prediction, self-correction, confirmation, and inferential thinking to interpret meaning beyond the print. Readers understand literary forms, author and illustrator styles, and the author's intent. They know how to set their own pace and purpose for the text in order to get the necessary information. Readers respond meaningfully and personally to literature. They learn new concepts and information from reading.

Similarly, in writing the writer's one aim is to convey his/her message in writing to an audience. In conveying this message the writer works at putting his/her voice into the writing. At the beginning stages, the writer is focused on forming letters and putting letters together (mechanics) so that someone else can read the message even though his/her message is a primary concern. As the writer becomes fluent in his/her ability to write the message, the focus then shifts to writing in various styles and forms. The writer learns to be able to write in a specific style or form so that his/her intent is most effectively conveyed. The ability to adjust style and form to fit the intent is a characteristic of a mature writer.

Writing development parallels reading development. Writing and reading enhance each other when taught together. Students can learn from reading certain aspects that will influence their writing. An example of this is when the students read several books by one author. Studying the author's style will sometimes influence the students' in their writing. They will want to write a piece using this author's style. The same holds true for writing. Students find that by writing their own pieces they realize the importance of organization or audience and observe these aspects as they read.

In whole language, to develop these attitudes and behaviors during the primary grades (K-3) where learning to read and write is experienced, the teachers find it beneficial to break up the process into stages. In New Zealand, the stages are known as Emergent, Early, and Fluency. In our school district, we adapted and defined these stages and added one (Pre-Emergent) to assist teachers in understanding and providing instruction to primary grade children.

In understanding these three stages of literacy development an analogy might be drawn from how one learns to drive a car. In the very beginning, one is aware that there are cars and their purpose, travel (Pre-Emergent) . Then, being in a car going some place, perhaps pretending to drive a car as a child or in the car driving simulator, one develops the awareness of what it's like to drive a car. The person is "emerging" into the role of a driver (Emergent). Next, the person takes lessons and gets a driver's permit. During this period of learning to drive the person is consumed with the mechanics and maneuvers of the car and usually drives around their hometown which is familiar territory. Until the mechanics and maneuvers become automatic, it is difficult to drive in unfamiliar areas (Early stage). Having passed the driver's test indicating that the person is competent in mechanics and maneuvers, the driver is ready for unfamiliar territory and application of these mechanics and maneuvers (Fluency stage). The learning to read/write process is parallel in nature. However, this learning to read/write process generally takes the first three to four years of school. One must keep in mind that the pace of development is dependent on the child, his/her capabilities, and the literacy experiences provided in school and at home.

Pre-Emergent Stage

The **pre-emergent stage** is characterized by a child becoming aware of print and writing in his/her world. For most children this stage takes place before entering school, but for deprived children school can be the first time that they encounter print or writing of any kind. Holdaway (1979) speaks of a literacy set in which the factors of motivation (expectation from print), linguistics (being familiar with language in written form), operations (strategies for understanding written language), and orthography (knowledge of print conventions) influence the child as he/she proceeds through the stages of reading and writing. Children at the pre-emergent stage are curious about books and print. They are familiar with book language and use some in their spoken language. They understand that stories have a beginning, middle, and end and can predict some of the language in books. They also understand that there are symbols involved in print and perhaps how a book reads (ex: front cover begins a story).

In addition, the child can successfully communicate a spoken message and can be reasonably assured that the message will be understood according to his/her intent.

Reading

The child has experienced books through the bedtime stories, videos, audiotapes, and storytelling.

An interest in books has developed and some of the child's favorites can be recited from memory.

The child is familiar with some forms of print in association with environmental print (ex: MacDonald's).

Writing

The child has also experienced some attempts at writing on his/her own such as scribbling or coloring.

The child is interested in writing his/her name or perhaps some letters or numbers.

Emergent Stage

The **emergent stage of reading** is where the child begins to experience print through books. Previous to this stage (Pre-Emergent) the child has been exposed to books through bedtime stories and environmental print. The child might also have had some writing experiences (picture drawing, scribbling). Now as an emergent reader the child can begin to take on the role of reader by "pretending" to read books read to him/her. That is, the child is able to remember the text in repetitious books or tell the story through the pictures, thereby pretending to read the text. Many good literature books are read to and with the child to instill in them the rewards of reading. Here are some more specific details of the emergent stage of reading:

- Child is learning to love books
- Child often pretends to read a book by using the pictures or "reading" memorized text especially of favorite books
- Child is strongly dependent on pictures as support in telling the story or reading the text
- Child can point to the spoken words of a book while someone else reads it or the child reads it
- Child begins to understand the conventions of print (ex: capitals, directionality, print vs. picture)
- Child enjoys using the rhythm, rhyme, and repetition of language

In the **emergent stage of writing**, the student begins to realize that those squiggly lines mean something and tries to imitate the writing by scribbling or attempting letters. The student's drawings are used to communicate a message but the student is trying to write to communicate. At this stage the child learns how to form letters and even though written at random, he/she can tell the story he/she has written. The student may also know from environmental exposure some familiar words and will write them in his/her piece even though the text is not appropriate for the story. Here are some more characteristics of writing at the emergent stage:

- Child is experimenting with writing by drawing pictures, scribbling, writing a few familiar words or writing some isolated letters to convey meaning
- Child is learning to form letters and that they represent language
- Child may write a string of letters to represent language or one

letter to stand for one word or phase
- Child can tell the story or message, but often the written symbols are not in a one-to-one correspondence with child's oral story

Early Stage

As the competencies of the emergent stage become evident, the child is ready to proceed to the early stage. As the child transitions into the **early stage of reading**, the child will begin to more readily notice the differences in words and recognize more conventions of print. The child while moving through this stage will learn the various cueing strategies and begin to use then effectively. The cueing strategies will become an effective tool in getting meaning from print. The main area of instruction in the early stage of reading is cueing strategies. This is the stage where the child learns to use these cueing strategies to get meaning from print. At the emergent stage, picture cues were most important but now the child is gradually progressing through four levels of the early stage in semantics (context/meaning), syntax (what type of word, ie. verb, noun; belongs where in a sentence because of our language structure), and graphophonics (letter/sound correspondence). At the end of this stage the child can readily use these cueing strategies and is able to read increasing longer pieces of literature. The characteristics of the early stage of reading are:

- Child is developing knowledge of words (sight vocabulary)
- Child is developing the ability to use the cueing strategies (picture cues, semantics, syntax, graphophonics) with ease
- Child can read short books on his/her own as long as pictures help to support text
- Child is developing a memory for longer text by listening to longer stories over time
- Child uses cueing strategies to try and figure out words unfamiliar to him/her
- Child confirms and self-corrects his/her attempts at figuring out unfamiliar words in reading

- Child begins to personally respond to books and learn from books
- Child is increasingly striving to get meaning from the text rather than relying on pictures
- Child uses picture cues as a check on his/her meaning derived from text

Students at the **early stage of writing** are making use of the sound/symbol relationship they've learned. Generally they begin by using initial and final consonant relationships in words such as bt for bat. Later in the early stage the vowels appear. The writing tends to be highly phonetic or in other words the students use predominately inventive spelling. The students do continue to use familiar words. In the area of sentence structure, the students can write complete thoughts but tend to use patterns in their writing of simple sentences. Later in the stage, they begin to write pieces that have some organization of beginning, middle, and end. They also use words that tend to describe more of their content. Below are listed some specific characteristics for the early stage of writing:

Beginning of Early Stage

- Child writes a string of letters to represent message with perhaps some letters actually corresponding to beginning sounds of words
- Child is beginning to demonstrate that the letters on the paper are corresponding to the oral message or story told

Middle of Early Stage

- Child tends to write groups of letters and will space them to represent words. Some letters represent the sounds in the words — mostly consonant sounds
- In writing on the topic, the child tends to list or use repetitive language structures such as I like ice cream, I like cake
- A one-to-one match between the child's message or story and the written representation is predominant

End of Early Stage

- Child spaces words of invented spelling and uses some punctuation correctly
- Conventional spellings of words are appearing more frequently
- The text of the writing is more readable and can communicate its message basically alone without the child's oral interpretation
- The child begins to use a variety of sentence structures in his/her writing

Fluency Stage

With the competencies of the early stage underway, the child is ready to practice his abilities with longer text, concentrate more on interpretation of the text, and explore other genres at the **fluency stage of reading**. The fluency stage not only emphasizes the appropriate application of the cueing strategies but requires the reader to refocus his attention to interpretation and higher level thinking about the text. Throughout the four fluency levels the reader does this reading through various genres, learning different literary forms and author styles. Some of the characteristics of the fluency stage are:

- The child has developed sight vocabulary which is expanding rapidly
- The child has the ability and is practicing the appropriate use of the cueing strategies to read unknown words
- The child reads a variety of genre and adjusts purpose and pace as he/she reads
- The child moves away from just getting what the text says to meaning beyond the print (interpretation)
- The child is using the text to gain information, confirm or deny his/her own viewpoints, and respond critically to the text
- The child's focus is on author's message and not print details unless meaning is lost

At the **fluency stage of writing**, the student's writing uses mostly conventional spellings of words and is developed around a beginning, middle, and end. Paragraphing is being attempted and a larger variety of sentences is being used. More complex sentence structures are being used and more descriptive language is used to create mental images for the readers. Students are aware of different genres and attempt to imitate them. Author styles are experimented with in the writing. The concern for a specific, clear message in the writing is the central focus. Other characteristics of the writing are:

- The child writes many words and sentences about his topic with ease
- He/she uses mostly conventional spelling but also inventive spelling in trying out new words
- The child is aware of authors' styles and different genres; s/he experiments with writing in these styles or genres.
- The grammar and punctuation is mostly correctly used

In conclusion, as the child experiences these stages of literacy, s/he learns to read and write. Now, let's look generally at the levels in these stages.

Literacy Levels

The stages of reading and writing development are defined further into levels for the Early and Fluency stages. Designating Pre-emergent and Emergent as levels, we have a total of ten Literacy Levels. In the next several chapters these literacy levels are discussed in detail with description, activities, and assessment features (benchmarks). These Literacy Levels have been helpful to our teachers in understanding the reading/writing development, assessing students' abilities, and as guidelines in instruction. It has been a helpful framework for instruction in the whole language approach.

Before the detailed descriptions are presented, sometimes it is helpful to see the Literacy Levels at a glance. The following chart first presents key areas in the levels in terms of reading and then in terms of writing.

Literacy Levels

Key Reading Areas for Each Literacy Level

Pre-Emergent (Pre-Em)

-Awareness of print in environment
-Oral retelling of story or event
-Pretend reads a familiar book
-Enjoys being read to

Emergent (Em)

-Role of reader
-Conventions of print
-Print tells a story
-Pictures help to tell the story

Early 1 (E 1)

-Pictures help to tell the story
-Print tells a story
-Conventions of print
-Cueing strategies of meaning and language structure

Early 2 (E 2)

-Conventions of print
-Print tells a story with pictures
-Sight vocabulary developing
-Cueing strategies of meaning, language
  structure, sound/symbol

Early 3 (E 3)

 -Message is in the print
 -Sight vocabulary rapidly developing
 -Cueing strategies of meaning, language
  structure, sound/symbol
 -Becoming independent in reading

Early 4 (E 4)

 -Message is in the print
 -Developed sight vocabulary
 -Cueing strategies of meaning, language
  structure, sound/symbol well developed
 -Becoming independent in reading
 -Responses/shares reading experiences

Fluency 1 (F 1)

 -Begins to take an active role in interacting
  with author
 -Responses/shares reading experiences
 -Cueing strategies are automatic

Fluency 2 (F 2)

 -Active role in interacting with author
 -Begins to make interpretations about text
 -Uses own experiences to respond to text
 -Cueing strategies are automatic

Fluency 3 (F 3)

 -Engaged with author
 -Interprets text using experiences

-Reads for meaning and to learn from text
-Sharing/responding to text using experiences

Fluency 4 (F 4)

-Reads many different styles, authors, forms
-Interprets text using experiences
-Reads for meaning and to learn from text
-Independently reads, responds, and shares

Key Writing Areas for Each Literacy Level

Pre-Emergent (Pre-Em)

-Draws a picture to communicate a message
-Scribbles or attempts to write
-Writes name or a few letters

Emergent (Em)

-Uses random letter to communicate a message
-Reads own writing and tells story
-Writes letters of the alphabet

Early 1 (E 1)

-Uses some initial letters of words to communicate message
-Uses some familiar words to communicate
-Illustrations relate a definite story

Early 2 (E 2)

-Uses inventive spelling to communicate
-Writes simple, repetitive sentences
-Uses some punctuation/capitalization

Early 3 (E 3)

    -Beginning to write summaries of books read
    -Writing stories with beginnings and somewhat of an
     ending
    -Uses inventive and some conventional spelling

Early 4 (E 4)

    -Stories have a beginning, middle, and end
    -Descriptive words are being used for clarity
    -Uses some variety in sentence structure
    -Inventive and conventional spelling becoming more balanced

Fluency 1 (F 1)

    -Able to write on a topic and maintain focus
    -Story has a beginning, middle, and end
    -Uses a variety of simple sentence structures

Fluency 2 (F 2)

    -Becoming more detailed in writing
    -Uses descriptive language in writing
    -Conventional spelling is dominant

Fluency 3 (F 3)

    -Beginning to expand into different forms of writing
    -More development can be seen in the beginning, middle,
     and end of writing
    -Uses more complex sentence structure

Fluency 4 (F 4)

    -Beginning, middle, and end of story is well developed
    -Can support writing with details
    -Can imitate an author or genre
    -Uses complex sentences

Many educators will see these Literacy Levels as an adaptation of the basal reader. Moreover, the question often asked of these levels is how are they different from the basal reader. This important question will be explored next.

Comparison of the Basal Reader and Literacy Levels

The basal reader was developed based upon the premise that children needed to learn one skill first and then another skill. The levels of the basal are exclusive but dependent on each other. The skills and vocabulary of one level are necessary for the next. Here is a figure expressing that concept.

The readability of each level of the basal becomes increasingly more difficult.

3^2
3^1
2^2
2^1
1^2
Primer
Preprimer
Readiness

This is not the case with the Literacy Levels. Each Literacy Level has specific behaviors and strategies which are practiced by all good readers and writers. These levels are interdependent. The reader/writer will need to demonstrate these behaviors or strategies in order to develop into a proficient reader/writer. The following figure shows this concept.

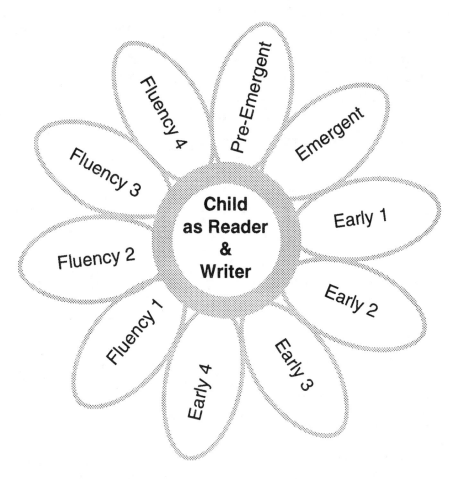

Moreover, the Literacy Levels in terms of reading books become more difficult in readability of text but not like the basal. The emergent books are easiest but the beginning early levels (E1 & E2) are similar in difficulty. The Early 3 and 4 books represent the next level of difficulty with Fluency 1 and 2 coming after them. The most difficult books are in the Fluency 3 and 4 levels but their readability is quite close. Furthermore, the Literacy Levels were defined based on behaviors and strategies necessary to read a specific book, not exclusively readability.

In summary, the behaviors and strategies present at each Literacy Level work together to build the foundation of reading and writing.

Fluency 1	Fluency 2	Fluency 3	Fluency 4
Early 1	Early 2	Early 3	Early 4
Emergent			
Pre-Emergent			

In order to effectively utilize these levels in instruction it is important to understand the typical learning pace of these competencies in the primary grades and the comparison between the components of whole language, the Literacy Levels and grade level. These charts are only a guideline for teachers and are not meant to be followed ridgedly. These comparisons are based on the idea that we are looking at the average child with average ability. In the case of higher-ability children, these comparisons are too low. In the case of below-average children, these comparisons are too high. These comparisons are given in the case of ideal conditions.

The following chart illustrates where a child with average reading ability would be instructed in the various primary grades. It also indicates the amount of time required by students to acquire the competencies in reading at each Literacy Level.

Comparison of Literacy Levels and Grade Levels

Grade Level	Literacy Levels	
Kindergarten	Em (Emergent)	April, May, June
Grade 1	Em, E 1, E 2	Sept. to Jan.
	E 3	Feb. to May, June
Grade 2	E 3 and/or E 4	Sept. to Jan.
	F 1 and F 2	Feb. to June
Grade 3	F 3 and F 4	Sept. to Jan.
	Beyond F 4	Feb. to June

This chart compares literacy level, whole language component, and grade level for average ability students. Depending on the teacher's purpose for instruction, s/he can select books and/or strategies at the appropriate literacy level for his/her grade level to use during a particular whole language component.

Literacy Levels Chart and
Whole Language Components

Read To: Teacher selects books according to appropriateness for grade level, theme, purpose, or language development.

Shared Reading

Kindergarten	Grade 1	Grade 2	Grade 3
PreEm Em E1	E2 E3 E4 F1	F1 F2 F3 F4	F4 Beyond F4

Guided Reading/Writing Development

Kindergarten	Grade 1	Grade 2	Grade 3
PreEm Em	Em E1 E2 E3	E4 F1 F2 F3	F3 F4 Beyond F4

Independent Reading/Writing

Kindergarten	Grade 1	Grade 2	Grade 3
	Em E1 E2	E3 E4 F1	F2 F3 F4

In the next three chapters the ten Literacy Levels are defined with activities for instruction and benchmarks for assessment. At the beginning of the Literacy Level will be a description of the level followed by more specific reading and writing behaviors characteristic of that level.

After the specific behaviors of reading and writing, the focus areas of that level are listed. Next is the general instructional format for reading because teachers will want to change their method of teaching for each level to encourage development of reading. This format can be applied in the Shared Reading or Guided Reading experience.

In order to develop the writing behaviors in depth at each level, the teacher would plan Guided Writing or Independent Writing experiences with the children, therefore, an instructional format for writing is not listed. However, the suggested activities to encourage the behaviors of the Literacy Level include reading and writing activities because reading and writing enhance each other.

Finally, the benchmarks for assessment are listed. These benchmarks are useful in determining whether the student has acquired the competencies of the Literacy Level and is ready to be challenged by the next Literacy Level.

Before moving on to the detailed descriptions of the Literacy Levels, it is important to discuss two aspects of the learning-to-read process which are mentioned throughout the Literacy Levels: conventions of print and segmentation.

Conventions of Print and Segmentation

Learning to speak a language, children become aware of sounds of the language and use them to speak. They develop their language into complex sentences and can readily communicate their messages to others.

When children learn to read and write, they need to understand that language in written form has visual representations for the spoken language. In order to be able to be conversant in the language of reading and writing, children need to understand visual signals of language called conventions of print.

Marie Clay (1979) discusses the conventions of print and even has a test (Concepts About Print) which she used in her studies of beginning reading development. Conventions of print include: understanding the direction reading goes (left to right and return), the purposes for the marks of punctuation, print has separations defined as words and letters, etc. All of these conventions are important for beginning readers to understand. In the Literacy Levels these conventions are listed in the behaviors of the levels and as benchmarks for assessment. Several activities at each level address the conventions of print.

In addition, children require an understanding that language, when represented in reading and writing, is divided into parts called words, syllables, and sounds. This awareness of the language parts will be referred to as word segmentation, syllable segmentation, or sound segmentation. This ability to segment the language is crucial for being able to break the code of reading and for the spelling of words. Word and syllable segmentation helps facilitate voice-print match and the recognition that print uses words as one unit of division on the page.

Since sound/symbol development requires an awareness of sounds in the language (sound segmentation), unless this ability is present the effectiveness of sound/symbol instruction is significantly reduced. Griffith and Olson (1992) discuss sound segmentation or phonemic awareness in their article, "Phonemic Awareness Helps Beginning Readers Break the Code." According to this article, the concept that language is broken down into sounds is important for children in learning to read and spell words. Diane Sawyer (1987) has developed an assessment for this concept of segmentation: Test of Awareness of Language Segments (TALS). This test assesses word, syllable, and sound segmentation and is suggested for verification of these abilities in the Literacy Levels.

In our language arts program, these two areas have been found to be a vital part of learning to read and write. These concepts are developed and assessed throughout the Literacy Levels. They are key players in the learning-to-read/write process.

Summary

1. The general stages of Pre-Emergent, Emergent, Early, and Fluency are presented for an overview of the Literacy Levels.

Pre-Emergent: Stories and pictures go together. Child is aware that writing exists.

Emergent: There is print and it has meaning. Child attempts writing.

Early: Child has knowledge and use of various cueing strategies to help him/her get meaning from print. Child can write so the invented spelling is readable with some conventional words. With the development of the use of the cueing strategies the child is ready and capable of tackling longer and more complex print. In writing the child is ready to try different forms and use more specific language.

Fluency: The child's concentration is on learning from reading rather than deciphering print. Understanding the author's message requires more interpretation on the reader's part. The child can write a cohesive, organized, and readable writing piece.

2. The Literacy Level framework is presented as compared to whole language components and grade levels. These comparisons are only guidelines for teachers as they transition into whole language.

3. Two vital areas to the Literacy Levels are conventions of print and language segmentation.

Chapter 10   Pre-Emergent and Emergent Literacy Levels

PRE-EMERGENT LEVEL

The pre-emergent Literacy Level is characterized by an awareness of print and the use of print. Before children independently read or write a story, they are focused on the acquisition of oral language and the awareness of print. The children are expanding their oral vocabularies and learning about the world in which they live . They are becoming curious about books and enjoy having favorite books read again and again. Sometimes the children even memorize their favorite stories and "read" along with the adult. The children will often draw pictures to tell a story or tell a story from the pictures. The activities at the pre-emergent level usually take place in preschool or in the fall of the kindergarten year.

Pre-Emergent Behaviors of Reading and Writing

Reading	*Writing*
Can orally retell a story or event.	Can draw a picture that is recognizable.
Can orally converse with others.	
	Can explain or tell a story about picture.
Able to listen attentively to a read aloud story.	
	Scribbles or attempts to write on paper and refers to it as writing.
Interested in selecting a book to have read aloud.	

Reading	Writing
Returns to familiar books for another read aloud or to look at.	Can write name or a few letters.

Reading

Returns to familiar books for another read aloud or to look at.

Pretends to read familiar book.

Knows that print exists and understands that it is different than pictures.

Beginning awareness of word and syllable segmentation.

Writing

Can write name or a few letters.

Focus Areas for Pre-Emergent Level

1. Listening and following the pictures as stories are read

2. Oral language development

3. Awareness of print in books and environment

4. Telling a story from illustrations

5. Drawing pictures to tell a story

6. Attempts writing

General Instructional Format for Reading

At this level the teacher gathers the children around her/him for the read aloud book. The comfortable, relaxed setting provides the children with a warm feeling about being read to. The teacher reads aloud short, simple books which are often repetitive. That is, phrases or verses are repeated in a rhymical manner. Children will often chant or read along with the teacher these repetitive parts. The teacher encourages the children to become part of the story and discusses the story with the children. The teacher will often ask the children to retell the story in their own words.

Suggested Activities to Encourage Behaviors at Pre-Emergent Level

1. Reading aloud books with simple plots to encourage the retelling of the story in the child's own words and pretend rereading of the book.

2. Reading aloud of nursery rhymes or other rhyming verse to encourage repetition, memorization, and a "reading together" of text language.

3. Using wordless books to promote the child's telling of the story in his/her own language. The teacher might model this process first by demonstration. This activity is also a good one for language experience (See Chapter 6). The children can see their telling of the wordless story in print.

4. Providing read along tapes of simple stories for small groups of children.

5. Use finger plays, tapping or clapping to rhythmically read through story. These activities assist children in understanding word and syllable segmentation.

6. Using a simple big book as a read aloud book to show print and picture difference.

7. Have the children help the teacher label various objects around the room. This activity will encourage their writing attempts.

8. Encourage the children to label their drawings, even with only one letter.

Benchmarks of Acquisition for the Pre-Emergent Level

Reading

1. Identifies the front of book.

2. Knows the difference between print and picture.

3. Can find a familiar book and pretend read.

4. Can follow a story as the teacher reads aloud or with a read along tape by turning pages at appropriate time.

5. Some word and syllable segmentation is evident.

6. Enjoys selecting books of interest on own to look at and "read" the pictures.

Writing

7. Attempts some writing (a letter or a word).

8. Orally tells a story from pictures.

9. Can reread individual language experience sentence.

Assessment Procedures for Pre-Emergent

Assessment at this level is informal and observed. The teacher asks the child to show her/him the front of a book and point to the print of the book. The child follows along with the teacher as s/he reads by knowing when to turn the pages and/or from which page the teacher is reading. The teacher observes the child pretend reading a familiar book and selecting books of interest to picture read.

The teacher gives the child some short sentences and asks the child to use blocks to represent the words s/he "hears" in the sentence. The child is also given two-syllable and three-syllable words to represent parts with the blocks. This activity is short and non-threatening. The teacher also observes the child writing a letter or word.

When the teacher observes these behaviors, they are dated on the Benchmark Chart (See Appendix).

EMERGENT LEVEL

At this level, the child begins to learn about print. The child begins to understand that print conveys a message. The child begins to develop the attitude that s/he can read and that the text can be returned to and will say the same thing. This level introduces children to the world of books that they can begin to read on their own.

In writing, the child begins to use letters to convey a message. The child can often read his/her message even though there are only some random letters.

Emergent Behaviors of Reading and Writing

Reading	*Writing*
Can understand that print communicates a message.	Writes on own using random letters.
Can locate print on page.	Can read own story after writing it, even though text is random letters.
Can find familiar words in text.	May use familiar words in writing.
As child reads emergent books, can voice-print match.	Can identify and form letters of alphabet.
Can reread individual language experience stories with voice-print match.	Uses illustrations to tell a story.
Can reread individual language experience story by remembering words.	
Can recognize period, question mark, and explain purposes of punctuation.	
Can identify the difference between capital and small letters.	

Emergent Behaviors of Reading and Writing

Reading   *Writing*

Can find the capital and its matching small letter in text.

Can orally rhyme words.

Understands the left to right direction and return sweep of text reading by pointing and following along.

Orally can summarize a book read.

Can count the number of words in a sentence in the book.

Can segment at the word and syllable level.

Can use a picture cue to assist in reading. Uses pictures to assist in reading the words.

Can reread emergent level books with expression, ease, and enjoyment. Book has been read with teacher.

Enjoys being read to and listens attentively with understanding.

Can predict story topic by cover picture and title.

Developing own specific interests in books.

Focus Areas for Emergent Level

1. Conventions of print:
   a. where print is located
   b. how you move while reading (directionality)
   c. capitalization and punctuation recognition and meaning
   (period, question mark)
   d. voice-print match using emergent books

2. Word and syllable segmentation.

3. Reading communicates a message.

4. Letters can be used for writing to assist in communicating.

5. Reading and writing are enjoyable.

General Instructional Format for Reading (based on 3 - 5 instructional sessions per book)

1. At the emergent level, the teacher will distribute the books and ask the children to find the cover. The teacher will ask the children to point to the title and the teacher will read the title. S/he will ask the children to look at the cover picture, listen to the title, and predict what the story might be about.

2. The teacher reads the book to the children. The children follow along by pointing to the words as the teacher reads.

3. Together the children and teacher read the book. Children and teacher point to words as they read.

4. Teacher and children discuss meaning of the book. Children reread the book with support from teacher.

5. Teacher selects specific behaviors to work on with children from list depending on abilities of children and book selected. S/he provides reinforcement on these behaviors/strategies using a game, worksheet, or writing task.

6. Teacher selects activities for children to do with book from suggested activities list.

Suggested Activities to Encourage Behaviors at Emergent Level

1. Using big books or small books — one copy for each child to read along with the teacher — develop conventions of print. That is, the teacher and children can point to punctuation and/or capitalization for identification and purpose. The picture cues to help tell the story are also important to emphasize at this level. The teacher and students should also point to each word as spoken. This behavior assists word segmentation and voice print match.

2. Teacher and children can rewrite the book together. By rewriting a book the teacher rewrites the stems or sentence structure of the text. As a group the teacher and children fill in the characters and events to rewrite the book into a new story with similar structure but different content.

For example: *King Bidgood's in the Bathtub* by Audrey Wood (New York: Harcourt, Brace, Jovanovich, 1985) becomes Queen Witch is in the Bathtub, a Halloween story. The children share in drawing the pictures to match the developed text. This rewrite can be used as a big book or small group for the purposes of conventions of print, rereading together, etc. This activity promotes text language awareness, print communicates a message, conventions of print, how books are written, and enjoyment of reading.

3. The teacher's written language experience stories for group or individual is helpful in promoting voice-print match, print awareness, and word segmentation.

4. Child can practice writing individual letters of the alphabet (capital and small) by teacher selecting words for child to find in emergent book. The child writes the beginning letter down by naming it. Teacher assists child in letter formation and introduces the sound of the letter.

5. Child is asked to draw a picture of an event in the story, a favorite part of the story, or a different ending to the story. The child then writes describing the picture or the teacher can use the language experience technique to write the description.

6. Word and syllable segmentation activities can be done both in large and small groups. These include tapping out words of sentences, moving to rhythmic language, clapping out syllables in words, cutting up sentence strips into words, and using the word cards of a sentence to put the words in the appropriate order for the sentence.

7. Activities or games in rhyming can be used to develop an awareness of sounds and rhyme in the language.

8. The teacher selects poems, books, etc. for choral speaking which show the rhythm of language.

9. In sharing or guiding a book, the teacher reads aloud sentences and stops. S/he has students fill in a word that fits the context of the words in print.

10. Children need time to write on their own daily. At this level, the teacher will need to assist them in their writing by helping them to distinguish sounds and letter representations of those sounds.

11. Children can write their own books if the teacher develops blank pages with a sentence stem on it such as "I like ____ " on each page. The children will write in their response and draw a picture showing their choice.

Benchmarks of Acquisition for Emergent Level

Reading

1. Understands how reading goes (left to right).

2. Understands which part and which page of print is read first.

3. Can voice-print match using the emergent book.

4. Identifies and explains purpose of period and question mark.

5. Can identify a capital letter in a sentence.

6. Understands where the first and last part of a sentence is.

7. Can word and syllable segment (Use TALS [Sawyer, 1987] to verify).

8. Orally can summarize book read.

9. Enjoys being read to and listens attentively.

10. Using the picture and title on the cover of the book, can predict what story will be about.

11. Enjoys rereading emergent books.

12. Developing specific interests in books and selects them on own to read pictures.

Writing

13. Attempting to convey a message by writing, usually random letters but may have some sound/symbol correspondence.

14. Draws pictures to convey a message.

15. Tries to label pictures or writes a message using a few letters or known words like cat, dog, mom, and dad.

Assessment Procedures

1. Children are asked to read together with the teacher an emergent level book not read before. Before they read the book, the teacher asks the children to predict what the story is about from the title and cover picture. As they are reading, the children should be able to point to the words easily as the teacher reads (voice-print match item) Next, the teacher asks them to summarize the book orally by asking what the book was about.

2. As the children are reading the book with the teacher, the teacher observes whether the children move in the left to right direction and know which page to read first.

3. The teacher asks the children individually to point to a period and question mark. S/he also asks each child the purpose for the period and question mark. Children usually respond with "It tells you when to stop." and "It asks a question."

4. The teacher asks the children to point to the first and last part of a sentence and a capital letter.

5. The teacher individually administers the TALS (Sawyer, 1987) Parts A and B to verify word and syllable segmentation or develops her/his own assessment of these abilities.

6. The teacher observes whether the children enjoy rereading emergent books,

enjoy being read to and listen attentively, and are developing an interest in certain books.

7. The teacher observes the child's drawings and writing. The teacher observes if some writing is evident and if the child can orally tell the story of his/her picture.

All of the above items are checked off on the Benchmark Record Keeping Chart (see Appendix).

Note: If the child has difficulty with part of the items such as purpose of period, but has the majority of the benchmarks (segmentation must be passed) then the child can begin to develop the competencies at the next level. The teacher notes these failed items on the Benchmark Chart (see Appendix) and continues to work on them in Early 1. The teacher can retest on those items when the child has demonstrated knowledge.

Summary

The Pre-Emergent and Emergent Levels of Literacy were discussed in this chapter. The key areas for these levels are:

Key Reading Areas

Pre-Emergent (Pre-Em)

-Awareness of print in environment
-Oral retelling of story or event
-Pretend reads a familiar book
-Enjoys being read to

Emergent (Em)

-Role of reader
-Conventions of print
-Print tells a story
-Pictures help to tell the story

Key Writing Areas

Pre-Emergent (Pre-Em)

-Draws a picture to communicate a message
-Scribbles or attempts to write
-Writes name or a few letters

Emergent (Em)

-Uses random letter to communicate a message
-Reads own writing and tells story
-Writes letters of the alphabet

Chapter 11 Early Literacy Levels

In learning to read, one focus of the early reading levels is cueing strategies or how to pronounce unfamiliar words. The cueing strategies emphasized are semantics (meaning), syntax (language structure), picture cues, and sound/symbol (phonics). Another focus is understanding the author's message. The child learns that text has meaning and tells the story. There are four levels in the early stage in which the student gradually acquires these competencies.

EARLY 1 LEVEL

At the Early 1 level, the child continues to gain confidence as a reader but now must pay closer attention to individual words. The child begins to learn individual words and is able to recognize them in other books. The child understands that print is telling the story and can identify the general topic of the book. The child begins to use prediction as a strategy in understanding the author's message. The child also knows that our language has words and syllables represented in print or word and syllable segmentation. The child becomes aware that letters have specific sounds. The child begins to use initial and final sounds to assist in his/her writing.

Early 1 Behaviors of Reading and Writing

Reading

Can voice-print match text with more than one line of print as teacher reads.

Can identify when words or lines of print are read out of sequence.

Can take a cut-up sentence (into words) from story and put words in appropriate order.

Can identify the differences in words in text using configuration and initial letter.

Can auditorily distinguish initial and final sounds in words. Medial sounds may be atttached to the initial or final sounds.

Can isolate letters within words upon request and understands first and last letter of a word concept.

Can identify word changes in Early 1 books (i.e. can see when the words are different).

Applies initial/final consonant sounds (letter to sound, sound to letter).

Writing

Uses random letters to write mostly but now can use initial consonant to designate some words.

Can rewrite a book on own if given an emergent book format and fill in blank. (Example: " I can read to _____ . " Picture will clarify blank word.

Uses some familiar and word bank words in writing.

Illustrations show a definite story.

Early 1 Behaviors of Reading and Writing

Reading   *Writing*

Can substitute initial consonants when rhyming words.

Can identify some words by sight.

Shows knowledge and demonstrates that left page is read before right and top text is read before bottom in books.

Demonstrates an understanding of the first part of a sentence and last part of a sentence.

Can use a picture cue to assist in reading an unfamiliar word.

Can use pictures to predict and understand story line.

Can identify comma, exclamation point, and quotation marks and explain purposes of punctuation.

Can independently read emergent level books with minimal support from teacher.

Can orally summarize book to teacher. (What is book about?)

Begins to understand inflectional endings and contractions.

Focus Areas for Early 1 Level

1. Begin to distinguish between words using configuration and initial letter.

2. Begin to develop sight vocabulary.

3. Able to voice-print match the book read with the ability to distinguish when lines/words are out of sequence.

4. Begins to apply initial and final sounds in reading.

5. In writing, beginning to use initial letter to convey a message.

General Instructional Format for Reading (based on 3 - 5 instructional sessions per book)

1. At the Early 1 level, the teacher will ask the children to point to the title and the teacher will read the title. S/he will ask the children to look at the cover picture, listen to the title, and predict what the story might be about. The teacher will distribute the books and ask the children to follow along by pointing to the words as s/he reads the story.

2. The teacher reads the book to the children. The children follow along by pointing to the words as the teacher reads.

3. Together the children and teacher read the book again. Children and teacher point to words as they read.

4. Teacher and children discuss meaning of book. Children reread book with support from teacher.

5. Teacher selects specific behaviors to work on with children from list depending on abilities of children and book selected. S/he provides reinforcement on these behaviors/strategies using a game, worksheet, or writing task.

6. Teacher selects activities for children to do with book from suggested activities list.

Suggested Activities to Encourage Behaviors at Early 1 Level

1. When the teacher is reading the text, children can practice voice-print match by pointing to the words as the teacher reads. The teacher can read words or phrases not in print or skip over words as a game with the children to develop the awareness that print is specific and certain letters make up certain words. Another concept this activity develops is that the reader must focus in on the entire word while reading or meaning can be lost. Punctuation, especially comma, exclamation point, and quotation marks, and other conventions of print are identified and their purpose explained.

2. The teacher writes sentence strips of text in book. The sentence strips can be used for reordering the book. Each sentence can then be cut up by the children into words. After the words are mixed up, the children can reorder the sentence.

3. Rewriting emergent level format books can be fun. The student is given a prepared book like: My Like Book. On each page of the book the teacher has written: I like _____. The students put a word in the blank and draw a picture to correspond to the word. The word will probably be written in inventive spelling. Children can read these books to the others.

4. The children can draw a picture of a meaningful aspect of the story. In their own writing, they can describe the picture.

5. In order to develop the picture cueing strategy, the children need to be encouraged to use the pictures as they read the text. Using wordless books and having teacher-prepared sentence strips to match the picture is another activity to develop picture cues. The child would use the picture to read the sentence strip and assist in identification of unknown words.

6. The children are asked during shared or guided reading to find the first and last part of sentences, orally summarize the book, which page to read first, and where print is located.

7. The children can read emergent level big books or small books during independent reading time. They can also be encouraged to partner read these emergent books.

8. Sound segmenting activities are important at this level. These activities might include using markers such as blocks to represent sounds heard in a simple word spoken by the teacher. The teacher could also present a certain sound for the children to listen for in words like "m." The teacher then would say three words like: bike, mother, and coat. The children would be asked to identify the word with the sound of "m" at the beginning. Other sounds could be practiced in this way.

9. Using word families found in the book read can be useful to practice substituting initial consonants in words. For example: "Bat" is found in the book. The teacher has the children rhyme words with "bat" and asks for the initial consonant to write:

bat
_at
_at
_at

10. The teacher can begin to develop a sight word bank for the class (Shared Reading) and/or group (Guided Reading). As she/he develops this word bank, the teacher asks the children to locate the word in the text for part of the time and spell the word to her/him. For the other times, the teacher calls out the word for the bank and asks the children to give what consonants are indicated by the sounds in the word. The more difficult phonic elements such as vowels would be given by the teacher at this time.

Benchmarks of Acquisition for Early 1 Level

Reading

1. Can identify words from other similar words when the teacher pronounces the words to be identified.

2. Understands how reading goes when there is more than one line of print (left to right and return).

3. Orally can state the topic of the book read.

4. While reading, the student can use initial sounds to pronounce the unknown words.

5. Enjoys being read to and listens attentively to read aloud.

6. Can orally summarize read aloud book.

7. Can identify and explain use of comma, exclamation point, and quotation marks.

8. Beginning to predict the next part of the story while reading.

9. Able to recognize words in text by pointing when teacher gives orally.

10. Able to follow words in text while story is being read and recognizes when words or sentences are out of sequence.

11. Enjoys rereading Early 1 books independently and/or with a peer.

12. Can isolate one and two words and letters in print.

13. Can identify first and last letter of a word in book.

14. Can read emergent books independently (not first read with teacher) and understands message.

Writing

15. While writing, the student attempts to use initial sounds to write his/her words.

16. Can write a sentence using inventive spelling (medial letters or sounds are usually not present).

17. Attempts to convey a message through writing. Mostly letters are used that correspond somewhat to sounds in words.

Assessment Procedures

1. Children are asked to read together with the teacher an Early 1 level book not read before.

2. As the children are reading the book with the teacher, the teacher observes whether the children move in the left to right direction with a return sweep. S/he may pause at an unfamiliar word to see if the children can use initial consonants to assist in pronouncing unfamiliar words.

3. During the initial reading, the teacher will want to stop and ask the children what they think will happen next. The teacher is supporting the children in their use of prediction.

4. The teacher uses the book for assessment of the following benchmarks:
      -identify and explain comma, quotation marks, and exclamation
        point
      -identify words from similar words when pronounced by the

teacher (i.e. teacher puts the words " hit, hop, help" on the board; the child selects the word given by the teacher)

-identify words in text when given by teacher (i.e. teacher asks child to point to the word "make")

-identify words and letters in text given by teacher

-recognize words out of sequence in the text when read by the teacher

5. After reading the book, the teacher asks the children to tell what the book was about.

6. The teacher can observe during a read aloud book the attention and understanding of the book. S/he asks the child to orally summarize this book.

7. The teacher can also observe if the children can read an Emergent book independently and relate what it was about to the teacher.

8. Over time, the children will demonstrate to the teacher their interest and enjoyment in books.

9. From various writing pieces, the teacher can observe the progress in writing.

Note: If the child has difficulty with only a couple of items, such as punctuation or isolating words, then the child can move to the next level. The teacher notes these failed items on the Benchmark Record Keeping Chart (see Appendix) and continues to work on them in Early 2. The teacher can retest on those items when the child has demonstrated knowledge.

EARLY 2 LEVEL

Children are developing the ability to use the structure of their language, the picture cues, and the meaning of sentences to assist them in their reading. They are developing more words that they know on their own (sight vocabulary) and recognize in other texts. The children are fully aware at the end of this level of the sound/symbol connection but usually don't apply it yet. The children understand the message of the author and are able to summarize the story events. In writing, the children are using more letters to represent words (inventive spelling) and are using simple sentence patterns to convey their message.

Early 2 Behaviors of Reading and Writing

Reading

Can use meaning (semantics) and language structure (syntax) to figure out unfamiliar words.

Can use configuration to assist in figuring out unfamiliar words.

Beginning to apply initial and final sounds while reading when confronted with an unfamiliar word. Medial sounds are not necessarily attended to in reading at this time.

Can distinguish all sounds in simple words (sound segmentation).

Writing

Can write using inventive spelling (letters used correspond to some sounds in words).

Can write in a patterned structure. (ex: I like apples. I like peaches.)

Can write a short "story" (2-5 sentences) which is difficult to read but has one or more parts to the organization (either a beginning or maybe also an end).

Can use some punctuation in story but not consistently.

Early 2 Behaviors of Reading and Writing

Reading

Can use pictures to assist in self-corrections and confirmations while reading unfamiliar text.

Can remember some words by sight (sight vocabulary).

Can orally summarize book with some descriptive detail.

Can orally begin to give some sequential detail of book — perhaps beginning and ending.

Attempts to orally state problem-resolution or cause-effect in book.

Writing

Can use some capitalization appropriately.

Can write most sentences in appropriate language structure (subject and predicate).

Can rewrite an Emergent or Early 1 book independently.

Focus Areas for Early 2 Level

1. The child will demonstrate while reading that he/she is applying the meaning/picture cueing strategy (semantics) and the language structure cueing strategy (syntax).

2. While reading the child will begin to make use of initial and final sounds to determine an unfamiliar word in text and in writing.

3. Through the ability to sound segment words, the children become aware of the sound/symbol connection.

4. Child will use self-correction as a check on the use of the cueing strategies.

5. Child begins to develop a sight vocabulary.

6. The child is beginning to use punctuation and capitalization in reading and writing.

7. In writing, simple and patterned sentence structures are developed.

8. The children are encouraged to summarize the story events.

General Instructional Format for Reading (based on 3 - 5 instructional sessions per book)

1. At the Early 2 level, the teacher will ask the children to point to the title and the teacher will read the title. S/he will ask the children to look at the cover picture, listen to the title, and predict what the story might be about. The teacher will distribute the books and ask the children to read the book with her/him.

2. Together the children orally read the book again. Children and teacher discuss the meaning of the book.

4. The teacher selects some high frequency words to put on cards and flash to the students. This activity focuses on sight vocabulary.

5. The teacher selects specific behaviors to work on with children from the list depending on abilities of children and book selected. S/he provides reinforcement on these behaviors/strategies using a game, worksheet, or writing task.

6. The teacher selects activities for children to do with the book from suggested activities list.

7. The teacher will focus on sound segmenting activities with the children with every book.

Suggested Activities to Encourage Behaviors at Early 2 Level

1. At this level, taking the book that was read and developing a cloze exercise is helpful for applying semantics and syntax. A cloze exercise is one in which selected words are left out of a passage from the book. The children write a word in the blank that makes sense to them. This word does not have to be the exact word. Synonyms are acceptable. At this level, one word left out of a sentence from the

book is adequate. Children can complete this with the teacher in Shared Reading or in small groups in Guided Reading. In Guided Reading, each child completes an exercise.

2. Several sound segmenting activities are most helpful at this level (see Early 1 Activity number 8). In Guided Reading, children should be experiencing sound segmentation activities frequently.

3. Using sight vocabulary familiar to the children as well as vocabulary from the Early 2 book, the teacher writes sentences on sentence strips with the initial and/or final sounds of words missing. The children are asked to read the sentences and supply the missing letters. In Guided Reading, the child would work on this activity at some point independently. This activity helps to focus the child on initial and final sounds.

4. Sight vocabulary development is important at this level. The teacher will supply individual or group word banks for children at this time. Games such as word recognition bingo and word concentration are suggested to practice remembering these words.

5. During the initial reading of the Early 2 book, the teacher will encourage the child to read a sentence not yet read by the teacher. The teacher will observe whether the child is self-correcting using picture cues, semantics, syntax, configuration, and some sound/symbol to figure out unfamiliar words.

6. At this stage the books used usually have a story line. During the time the teacher is developing with the children the message of the author, an emphasis on story line and details of the story is useful. Children can be asked to orally describe or to write a sentence or two about the story events. Then the teacher can ask what happened in the story to support their summary (details).

7. To develop the ability to understand the problem/resolution or cause-effect in books, the teacher can construct a chart of title, author, problem, and resolution (cause, effect) and begin to list what the children discovered as they read the books. Over time this chart can be referred to for comparison and contrast.

8. Rewriting Emergent level or Early 1 books can be used to encourage attention to sentence patterns, capitalization, and punctuation.

9. Writing patterned simple-structured stories prepared by the teacher is suggested. For example: The teacher prepares a book called "I Like." Inside on the pages are patterned sentences with blanks for the children to write their own words. " I like _____."

10. The teacher can dictate to the children simple sentences for them to practice encoding or the sound/symbol strategy in writing.

Benchmarks of Acquisition for Early 2 Level

Reading

1. Using an Early 2 book, the child will be able to complete a cloze exercise of 5-7 sentences in length with one blank per sentence. The sentences are directly taken from the text (application of semantic and syntactic cueing strategies).

2. The child is able to sound segment or distinguish all sounds in a one — syllable word by using markers such as blocks. (Use Sawyer Test [Sawyer, 1987] to verify.)

3. Demonstrates understanding of story by orally expressing the story events.

4. Able to read 18 out of 20 familiar sight vocabulary words.

5. Often selects Emergent, Early 1, or Early 2 books to read on own.

6. Enjoys being read to and responds to story by relating own experiences to the read aloud story.

Writing

7. Uses inventive spelling to write a simple story.

8. Groups of letters are now being used to represent words. Many letters correspond to sounds in words.

9. Uses similar sentence patterns in writing such as "I like to eat. I like to swim."

Assessment Procedures

1. Children are asked to read together with the teacher an Early 2 level book not read before.

2. As the children are reading the book with the teacher, the teacher observes the children following along and reading aloud.

3. The teacher asks the children to reread orally the book. At this time s/he observes the children's use of cueing strategies. S/he also asks the children to relate the story events.

4. Next, the teacher asks the children to complete a cloze exercise prepared from the book read. The cloze exercise is usually 5-7 sentences in length with one blank per sentence.

5. The children demonstrate the awareness of sounds in words by either a teacher-developed activity or by the TALS (Sawyer, 1987), Part C, sound segmenting.

6. The teacher prepares a list of sight vocabulary words that the children have been learning. This list is administered individually to the children. An acceptable score is 18 correct out of 20, but the teacher needs to use her/his judgement.

7. Teacher observations of reading behaviors can indicate the children's enjoyment and interest in reading.

8. From various writing pieces, the teacher can observe the progress in writing.

Note: If the child has difficulty with only a couple of items, the teacher can use her/his judgement in deciding whether the child is ready for the challenges at the next level. The teacher can note any failed items on the Benchmark Record Keeping Chart (see Appendix) and continues to work on them in the next level. The teacher can retest on those items when the child has demonstrated knowledge. Passing sound segmenting is very important to Early 3. A child who has difficulty with sound segmenting will probably have difficulty with the sound/symbol strategy and spelling.

EARLY 3 LEVEL

The sound/symbol cueing strategy is focused on at this level. The children are ready to learn what sounds the various letters make, including single — vowel sounds. In addition, the child is beginning to use the text to summarize or retell rather than relying on pictures. They are developing more meaning from the text than what is in the pictures. Their sight vocabulary is developing rapidly now. Their writing skills are developing so that they are able to communicate more effectively in their writing. Their writing pieces are becoming more organized with a beginning and an end.

Early 3 Behaviors of Reading and Writing

Reading	Writing

Reading

Writing

Developing independent reading behaviors.

Knows that the text has more meaning than the pictures.

Can use sound/symbol as a strategy to figure out words.

Can apply knowledge of single vowels in figuring out unfamiliar words (ie. when sounding out words, generally uses appropriate vowel sound).

Understands that using meaning and language structure are the first strategies to use when coming to an unfamiliar word.

Can orally identify and retell story line of book.

Can orally identify the major character(s) in book.

Has several words in sight vocabulary and uses them in reading.

Can easily write in appropriate words in cloze exercise from book.

Responds to book by orally summarizing book and relating to own experiences.

Can write using inventive spelling with some conventional spelling.

Can write a story that has a beginning and an attempt at an ending.

Can write a general summary of guided or independent book (usually one sentence).

Can write a rewrite of Early 2 books.

Can respond to independently read books by writing a one-sentence response.

Beginning to use adjectives to clarify descriptions in writing.

Can write a general theme story (ex: all on playing games). Inconsistencies are common.

Becoming aware of authors' styles and attempting to copy them.

Use of sentence structure is becoming more varied.

Focus Areas for Early 3 Level

1. Ability to apply the sound\symbol strategy.

2. Orally retelling story line of a book with some detail.

3. Sight vocabulary development (usually develops at rapid pace).

4. Writing is beginning to be organized into a beginning and ending.

5. Message is in the text.

General Instructional Format for Reading (based on 3 - 5 instructional sessions per book)

1. At the Early 3 level, the teacher will ask the children to read aloud the story and will assist in unfamiliar words. This activity gives the children practice with using all the cueing strategies.

2. Children and teacher discuss the meaning of the book and begin to focus on story line.

4. Teacher selects some words from the story to put on cards. These words will be used by the children to practice decoding .

5. Teacher selects specific behaviors to work on with children from list depending on abilities of children and book selected. S/he provides reinforcement on these behaviors/strategies using a game, worksheet, or writing task.

6. Teacher selects activities for children to do with book from suggested activities list.

7. The teacher will focus on sound/symbol activities with the children with every book.

Suggested Activities to Encourage Behaviors at Early 3 Level

1. To focus on the beginning and ending of stories, the teacher can have the children rewrite the beginning or end of a story by changing setting, time, characters, etc.

2. Before reading the book, ask the children to only look at the pictures as the teacher or child turns the page. Then ask the children to orally or in writing express the story line of the book. Then have the teacher and children together read the book. Individually or as a group, the children can compare the two versions. The conclusion to be emphasized is that text has more meaning than pictures and that pictures can be used to get some meaning.

3. Sound/symbol is a major emphasis at this level. Since writing and dictation of sentences practices encoding or going from sound to print, here is an activity that focuses on going from print to sound. Both aspects of sound/symbol are important to develop.

This activity can be done with whole class, a small group, or an individual.

Step 1: Select appropriate words (words from reading that are basically phonetically regular). Appropriate words for your class or group would be those that the majority of students would not know by sight.

Step 2: Write the words on the board. Ask the children if they see any small parts, words, or syllables within the words that they already know. If they do, underline them and have students pronounce those particular parts. Ask the children who know the word not to pronounce it yet.

Step 3: Underline the phonetic sound parts of the word for the children. For example, underline blends, digraphs, vowel combinations, affixes, etc.

Step 4: Begin at the beginning of the word and sound out the parts of the word, asking the children to help you designate what the sounds of those underlined phonic elements are. After the word has been completely broken up into its sound parts, have the entire class repeat all of the sounds in sequence.

Step 5: The children as a class should be able to blend the sound elements together to form the correct word. Once the children are able to pronounce the word, the meaning should be briefly discussed and the word should be placed within an oral sentence.

This activity would take about 5-10 minutes and the teacher would probably select two words for each session.

4. Since sight vocabulary is developing at such a rapid pace in this level, the maintenance of a word bank becomes cumbersome. It becomes important at this level to observe the use of a sight vocabulary in reading. Therefore, the teacher can have children read the book aloud for the initial reading. This provides the opportunity for the teacher to observe children using the vocabulary they know and, of course, sounding out the unfamiliar words.

5. Continued discussion on plot and problem-resolution is encouraged. Another literary element is introduced: characters. The teacher can start by assisting children in the identification of major characters versus minor characters. Rewriting stories through the eyes of a major character or changing major characters are two suggestions. The teacher can also begin to chart characters and compare them in various stories.

6. The children are able to sound segment upon entering into this level. This level focuses on vowel sounds (long and short single vowels and r-controlled vowels) or medial sounds application. Some children may require direct practice in the form of word lists that alter the medial sound like:

    h__t (hot)
    h__t (hat)
    h__t (hit)
    h__t (hurt)
    h__te (hate)

The teacher gives the child the list with the missing medial sound. The teacher can call off the word, asking the child to put the medial sound they hear in the blank.

7. Cloze exercises become a regular activity in this level. Children are able to complete a cloze sentence from the Early 3 book with one word left out per sentence.

8. Writing dictated sentences can be helpful in determining the use and application of sound/symbol. It is important to start out with simple, short sentences and increase as the children become proficient.

9. Writing stories with a beginning and end are important at this level. The teacher can encourage this concept through language experience stories and by pointing it out in the books or stories the children read. The teacher would also model this concept in guided writing when the class writes a book or children write their own stories.

Benchmarks of Acquisition for the Early 3 Level

Reading

1. Can use sound/symbol relationship in dictated sentences presented by the teacher. These sentences are simple and contain words familiar to the child. (Can use Clay [1979] dictation sentences.)

2. Can complete a cloze exercise consisting of 7 sentences and one blank per sentence. These sentences are taken from the book read.

3. Can pronounce unfamiliar words in isolation (approximately 20). Some examples are: hint, wave, scrap, sport, and blame. The words follow long, short, and r-controlled vowel rules. This activity assesses one aspect of the graphophonic cueing strategy: the ability to apply sound/symbol relationship for phonetically regular words.

4. Can respond to book read by orally summarizing story and relating to own experiences.

Writing

5. Can write a simple story with an awareness of story sequence.

6. Uses inventive spelling and some conventional spelling to write a simple story.

7. Attempts to copy an author in writing.

8. Uses more description in writing to clarify message.

9. Uses some variety in sentence structure when writing.

Assessment Procedures

1. Children are asked to orally read the story. The teacher takes a running record (see Glossary) of the oral reading to assess the application of the cueing strategies.

2. The children and teacher discuss the meaning of the story. S/he asks the children to orally summarize the story and relate it to something in their own lives.

3. Next, the teacher asks the children to complete a cloze exercise developed from the story. It consists of about 7-9 sentences with one blank per sentence.

4. The teacher has the children individually read the prepared words having long, short, and r-controlled vowels. Usually scoring 18 correct out of 20 words indicates they can apply the sound/symbol strategy.

5. Lastly, the teacher reads one or two simple sentences for dictation. First the teacher reads them all at once and then slowly, a word or two at a time, for the children to write down. Clay (1979) has dictation sentences prepared for this purpose. The teacher uses this dictation sentence to assess the student's ability to use the sound/symbol strategy in writing.

6. From various writing pieces, the teacher can observe the progress in writing.

Note: If the child has difficulty with only a couple of items, the teacher can use her/his judgement in deciding whether the child is ready for the challenges at the next level. The teacher can note any failed items on the Benchmark Record Keeping Chart (see Appendix) and continues to work on them in the next level. The teacher can retest on those items when the child has demonstrated knowledge.

EARLY 4 LEVEL

In the Early 4 Level, the children are practicing and expanding the sound/symbol strategy with support from syntax, picture, and semantics. The vowel combinations are usually focused on at this level. The children are expressing the attitude that they can read almost anything now. They are understanding the author's message and are ready for longer, more difficult text. In writing, the children are developing their style and more organized, detailed writing pieces.

Early 4 Behaviors of Reading and Writing

Reading

Can usually use all cueing strategies (sound/symbol, semantics, syntax) appropriately.

Has knowledge of double vowel (i.e. ou, au, ew) and generally applies them when needed.

Can generally understand the author's message from text and uses pictures to clarify meaning.

Has the ability to carry simple story lines from page to page using memory.

Can identify contractions and understand their meaning and use.

Can understand author's message when sentence structures become somewhat more complex.

Can identify major characters in text and discuss attributes.

Can write summary of story plot.

Can identify setting and genre with teacher support.

Orally responds to book by relating own experiences.

Writing

Inventive spelling and conventional spelling are becoming balanced.

Written stories are generally showing a beginning, middle, and end.

Can use descriptive words inconsistently in writing to attempt at a more clear image.

Written topic is focused more on a general topic but digressions are common.

Uses more than one sentence structure in writing, but variety is limited and simple.

Can orally identify different styles of writing.

Focus Areas for Early 4 Level

1. Uses all cueing strategies in reading.

2. Understands author's message from text and uses pictures to clarify.

3. Student can write a summary of story plot.

4. Writing is being developed for organization, detail, and clarity.

General Instructional Format for Reading (based on 3 - 5 instructional sessions per book)

1. At the Early 4 level, the teacher will ask the children to sometimes read aloud the story and to sometimes read silently. This level practices silent reading. To practice careful silent reading, the teacher can give the children a purpose for the silent reading and then have them read orally the part that supports the teacher's questions.

2. Children and teacher discuss the meaning of the book and focus on understanding of the text.

3. Teacher selects some words with double vowel from the story to put on cards. These words will be used to practice decoding by the children.

4. Teacher selects specific behaviors to work on with children from list depending on abilities of children and book selected. S/he provides reinforcement on these behaviors/strategies using a game, worksheet, or writing task.

5. Teacher selects activities for children to do with book from suggested activities list.

Suggested Activities to Encourage Behaviors at Early 4 Level

1. The emphasis in the initial stage of reading these books is on oral reading by the children. The teacher is constantly observing and evaluating her readers to determine if they are applying all the cueing strategies. The application of cueing strategies is vital at this level.

2. The teacher presents and states the sound made by various double vowels found in the book. She asks the students to recall other words in which they have seen or heard the double vowels. The teacher also selects other words containing the double vowels for the children to practice decoding.

3. Another major emphasis at this level is the ability to understand the author's message. Some suggested activities to encourage this understanding is story webbing, charting of story events, a story plot time line, and a literary elements chart identifying major events, title, author, major characters, minor characters, problem, and resolution.

4.Students can write a summary of the Early 4 book read. The teacher has the children share their summaries. The teacher discusses what events were necessary in the summary to reflect the story. The children will probably need practice and support in this task.

5.Writing stories with a beginning, middle, and end can be practiced with teacher support. Topics can be suggested that relate to the books read.

6.Some development of the middle part of a story through the use of descriptive words and a variety of sentence structures is encouraged in writing. The Early 4 book can be the take-off point by identifying the use of adjectives and a variety of sentences in the book read. The children can practice this writing independently and then they can share and discuss their work with the group and teacher.

7. Contractions are a focus at this level. The child should be able to recognize contractions and explain their meaning. The teacher can identify them in the

books and chart them for the children. On the chart the teacher can list the contraction and what two words it stands for.

Benchmarks of Acquisition for Early 4 Level

Reading

1. Can orally respond to an Early 4 book by relating own experiences.

2. Can read an Early 4 book (not read before) and retell the story by writing unassisted.

3. Can demonstrate application of sound/symbol relationship by reading words following the double vowel rules. These words are not part of the sight vocabulary. Nonsense words may have to be used in this case. Examples: moat, awkward, mention, and outcast.

Writing

4. Writes a story with evidence of beginning, middle, and end.

5. Uses inventive spelling and conventional spelling.

6. Writes using descriptive words to clarify message.

7. Uses a variety of sentence structures in writing.

8. Developing an awareness of style in writing.

Assessment Procedures

1. Children are asked to silently read the story.

2. The children are asked to write a brief summary of the story read without the use of the book.

3. The teacher has the children individually read the prepared word cards to assess the application of the sound/symbol strategy. These words will all contain double vowels.

4. From various writing pieces, the teacher can observe the progress in writing.

Note: If the child has difficulty with only a couple of items, the teacher can use her/his judgement in deciding whether the child is ready for the challenges at the next level. The teacher can note any failed items on the Benchmark Record Keeping Chart (see Appendix) and continues to work on them in the next level. The teacher can retest on those items when the child has demonstrated knowledge.

Summary

The Early Literacy Levels were discussed in this chapter. The key areas for these levels are:

Key Reading Areas

Early 1 (E 1)

> -Pictures help to tell the story
> -Print tells a story

-Conventions of print
-Cueing strategies of meaning and language structure

Early 2 (E 2)

-Conventions of print
-Print tells a story with pictures
-Sight vocabulary developing
-Cueing strategies of meaning, language structure, sound/symbol

Early 3 (E 3)

-Message is in the print
-Sight vocabulary rapidly developing
-Cueing strategies of meaning, language structure, sound/symbol
-Becoming independent in reading

Early 4 (E 4)

-Message is in the print
-Developed sight vocabulary
-Cueing strategies of meaning, language structure, sound/symbol
  well developed
-Becoming independent in reading
-Responds to/shares reading experiences

Key Writing Areas

Early 1 (E 1)

-Uses some initial letters of words to communicate message
-Uses some familiar words to communicate
-Illustrations relate a definite story

Early 2 (E 2)

    -Uses inventive spelling to communicate
    -Writes simple, repetitive sentences
    -Uses some punctuation/capitalization

Early 3 (E 3)

    -Beginning to write summaries of books read
    -Writing stories with beginnings and somewhat of an
     ending
    -Uses inventive and some conventional spelling

Early 4 (E 4)

    -Stories have a beginning, middle, and end
    -Descriptive words are being used for clarity
    -Uses some variety in sentence structure
    -Inventive and conventional spelling becoming more balanced

Chapter 12   Fluency Literacy Levels

The fluency literacy levels continue the focus on getting the author's message, but with more complex and longer text the cueing strategies must be automatic. In these levels, the student is involved with interpretation and inference of text and higher level thinking skills. Various genre and other authors' styles become important aspects. The student's writing has developed his/her own style. The writing pieces are developed and appropriate for the audience.

FLUENCY 1 LEVEL

The Fluency 1 Level further develops the ability to get meaning from the text because the text is more complex. At this level the cueing strategies are becoming automatic. The reader slows down to focus on print only when meaning is lost. The children increase their understanding of the various literary elements common to literature. The students begin to develop their own style of writing and use more complex sentences to convey their message.

Fluency 1 Behaviors of Reading and Writing

Reading	*Writing*
Has a rapidly developing sight vocabulary.	Conventional spelling and inventive spelling are balanced.
Can use the four cueing strategies appropriately.	Written stories have a beginning, middle, and end with some development.
Can maintain understanding of author's message over longer pieces of text (chapters) using memory.	Uses descriptive words to help clarify writing.
Can read text with ease stopping only occasionally to decode words.	Uses a variety of simple sentence structures (subject + verb).
Uses text to understand author's message. Pictures are used for confirmation.	Uses a few (1-3) dependent clauses in writing (ex: When I go home, I eat a snack). When... home = dependent clause (more complex sentences).
Can write a summary of the plot.	Can write on topic with some digressions.
Attempts to use affixes, roots, and compound words to confirm unfamiliar words.	Develops own style of writing with teacher support.

Fluency 1 Behaviors of Reading and Writing

Reading   *Writing*

Can identify basic characters and describe their attributes by writing.

Can identify the problem/resolution, setting, and genre of a book.

Orally discusses climax of story with teacher support.

Can interpret text easily at literal level and visualize story in mind.

Begins orally to predict how things could be different in the story if character changed, event changed (playing w/meaning of text).

Orally responds to book, relating own experiences.

Focus in reading text is on meaning, not trying to figure out words.

Focus Areas for Fluency 1 Level

1. The focus while reading the book is on meaning, not trying to figure out words.

2. Identification of characters and development of character traits.

3. Story mapping of events in book.

4. Writing has organization and development.

General Instructional Format for Reading (based on 3 - 5 instructional sessions per book)

1. At the Fluency 1 level, the teacher will ask the children to read silently. This level practices understanding what is read silently. Sometimes the teacher will ask the student to read a passage orally to support an answer to a question.

2. Children and teacher discuss the meaning of the book and focus on understanding the text.

3. Sometimes the teacher can discuss vocabulary words if they are crucial to the understanding of the text and context is not helpful. Children can reinforce their cueing strategies with this activity.

4. Teacher selects specific behaviors to work on with children from list depending on abilities of children and book selected. S/he provides reinforcement on these behaviors/strategies using a game, worksheet, or writing task.

5. Teacher selects activities for children to do with book from suggested activities list.

Suggested Activities to Encourage Behaviors at Fluency 1 Level

1. At this level the child has been successful in developing the cueing strategies. Therefore, the purpose of oral reading — to observe the use of cueing strategies — is not a focus. Oral reading would now be used for oral expression or oral interpretation.

   The children are silently reading the story or chapter for initial reading. The teacher sets a purpose for reading to focus the reader and to practice changing the pace of reading depending on purpose. For example, if the teacher asks the children to read to remember the details of the story, the pace will be slower. If the teacher asks the children to read to determine the imagery brought to mind while reading, the pace is faster.

   The teacher will need to break the story or book into appropriate sections at this level if the text is too long to be read in one sitting.

2. As the teacher directs the comprehension questions through the text, the children are asked to read aloud the passage that supports their answers. Since the text at this level is basically at the literal level of understanding, many questions will focus on what happened in the story.

3. During the reading of the story the teacher can assist the children in keeping a story map, that is, summary statements about the book. This story map could be done at another setting from the reading to evaluate the children's ability to remember story plot.

4. The literary elements of plot, major characters, minor characters, setting, problem/resolution, and climax are identified together as a group. The children can identify characters and problem/resolution independently for the most part.

5. Affixes are becoming significant because of the more difficult vocabulary and the variety of genre being read. Words containing affixes can be listed from the story. The children should be able to use the context to figure out the meaning of these words with the teacher. Then, the teacher can discuss root word and affix-

es. Charting the affixes studied with their meaning would help to focus on these elements. Compound words can also be instructed in this way.

6. The teacher will want to select a variety of genres for the books. The children can begin to identify different types of books by having the teacher ask whether it's fiction or nonfiction. Then, the teacher can begin to identify mysteries, realistic fiction, poetry, information books, and fairy tales by discussing their characteristics. It will be helpful to study one genre at a time to develop these characteristics. The teacher can also guide the children in writing their own mystery, etc. after the characteristics have been identified and the children have seen models of it.

7. One aspect of a Fluency 1 story can be changed (event, character, etc.) and the students can rewrite it with a new aspect. Initially, the students will require teacher support for this activity.

8. The teacher can take sentences from the book and the students can rewrite sentences into different sentences or combine sentences. This activity will be helpful in developing more complex sentence structures. However, these rewritten sentences must have the same meaning.

Benchmarks of Acquisition for Fluency 1 Level

Reading

1. Can complete a cloze exercise of about 10 sentences with two blanks per sentence taken from the Fluency 1 level text read.

2. Reads a Fluency 1 book silently and completes story event sequence, that is, the teacher will ask the students to write the main events of the story in sequence.

3. Can identify major characters and list at least one attribute for each character.

4. Can orally respond to book by relating to own experiences.

Writing

5. Writing pieces have a beginning, middle, and end with some detail in the development.

6. Begins to use more complex sentences in writing.

7. Developing own style of writing.

Assessment Procedures

1. Children are asked to silently read the story.

2. The children are asked to write the main events of the story read without the use of the book.

3. The teacher asks the students to identify the characters (about 3 characters) and list an attribute for each character.

4. The students are asked to complete a cloze exercise developed from the story by the teacher. This cloze exercise has about 10 sentences taken from the book. Each sentence has two blanks.

5. The teacher asks the students to orally respond to the book and relate it to their lives.

6. From various writing pieces, the teacher can observe the progress in writing.

Note: If the child has difficulty with only a couple of items, the teacher can use her/his judgement in deciding whether the child is ready for the challenges at the next level. The teacher can note any failed items on the Benchmark Record Keeping Chart (see Appendix) and continues to work on them in the next level. The teacher can retest on those items when the child has demonstrated knowledge.

FLUENCY 2 LEVEL

At the Fluency 2 Level, the children are beginning to infer meaning from the text. That is, the children need to use their experiences to interpret what is being said at some points in the text. The children are continuing to develop their knowledge of literary elements and are beginning to read various genres on their own. Writing is developing through the use of vivid language. Details and more complex sentences are expanding the content of the writing.

Fluency 2 Behaviors of Reading and Writing

Reading

Writing

Uses text to understand author's message. Pictures are not necessary.

Conventional spelling is predominate but inventive spelling is still used.

Rereads text for meaning or interpretation.

Can develop at least one area (beginning, middle, end) in writing.

Able to infer from text.

Chooses descriptive language for clarity.

Uses own experiences to understand interpretation of author's message.

Uses mostly a variety of simple sentences that contain some dependent clauses usually of similar structure (ex: because..., when ...).

Begins to understand figurative language and humor in reading.

Generally can change manner and pace of reading for different genre.

Can write on topic and is beginning to focus on more specific aspect of topic.

Can rewrite story plot to summarize book.

Writing pieces are generally cohesive.

Uses affixes, roots, and compound words to confirm unfamiliar words.

Identifies in writing the problem/resolution of book.

Responds to text by writing how own experiences relate. Orally uses passages of book for support to response.

Focus Areas for Fluency 2 Level

1. Begins to infer meaning from text using own experience.

2. Able to briefly summarize the main events of the book.

3. Can use knowledge of affixes and compounds to confirm unfamiliar words in text.

4. Writing is more detailed and cohesive.

General Instructional Format for Reading (based on 3 - 5 instructional sessions per book)

1. At the Fluency 2 level, the teacher will ask the children to read silently. The teacher will often have students complete silent reading before coming to the group meeting.

2. Children and teacher discuss the meaning of the book from questions about the book. These questions are often given to the students to answer after they have read the book and before coming to the group.

3. Sometimes the teacher can discuss vocabulary words if they are crucial to the understanding of the text and context is not helpful.

4. Teacher selects specific behaviors to work on with children from list depending on abilities of children and book selected. S/he provides reinforcement on these behaviors/strategies using a game, worksheet, or writing task.

5. Teacher selects activities for children to do with book from suggested activities list.

Suggested Activities to Encourage Behaviors at Fluency 2 Level

1. Children at this level can begin to respond in writing to the text. At first the teacher will want the children to describe their favorite part of the story and why it's their favorite. Next, the teacher will want them to expand this discussion by comparing this favorite part to another favorite part of a different book. Furthermore, the teacher will ask the students to respond by relating their own experiences.

2. The teacher can point out and discuss the inferred aspects of the text. The teacher will want to get viewpoints from several students, encouraging the idea that interpretation is based on one's experiences as well as the text. The text can be used for support.

3. In addition to silently reading a portion of the text, the children can be asked to summarize in writing this portion and share it with the others.

4. Affixes are used by students at this level. The teacher might want to list a root word on the board and ask that the children add an affix to change the meaning of the word. This practice will assist the children in their own writing as well as reading.

5. Children can be asked to rewrite passages in the book, selecting and using more or different descriptive language to increase their knowledge of synonyms and adjectives. Also, this exercise will assist the children in writing with vivid, clear language. The teacher will probably need to demonstrate and support this exercise.

Benchmarks of Acquisition for Fluency 2 Level

Reading

1. Able to interpret with support from the book the meaning of the text.

2. Can complete a written cloze exercise that utilizes words with affixes as word choices.

3. Can briefly summarize the plot of the Fluency 2 book read silently.

4. Can write a response to text by relating own experiences and orally using passages from the book to support the response.

5. Can identify by writing the problem/resolution of a story.

Writing

6. Writing pieces are cohesive and use descriptive language to clarify message.

7. Develops at least one area of writing (beginning, middle, or end) using descriptive language, more complex sentences, and images to convey message.

8. Uses conventional spelling mostly but inventive spelling is still generally used.

Assessment Procedures

1. Children are asked to silently read the story.

2. The children are asked to interpret the meaning and show support by writing responses to these questions based on the text.

3. The teacher asks the students to briefly summarize the book.

4. The students are asked to complete a cloze exercise developed from the story by the teacher. This cloze exercise has about 7 sentences with word choices listed. These word choices utilize affixes.

5. The teacher asks the students to write a response to the book relating their own experiences and to write the problem/resolution. Then, the teacher asks the students to find parts of the book that support their responses.

6. From various writing pieces, the teacher can observe the progress in writing.

Note: If the child has difficulty with only a couple of items, the teacher can use her/his judgement in deciding whether the child is ready for the challenges at the next level. The teacher can note any failed items on the Benchmark Record Keeping Chart (see Appendix) and continues to work on them in the next level. The teacher can retest on those items when the child has demonstrated knowledge.

FLUENCY 3 LEVEL

The literary elements are developed in depth in Fluency 3. Inference or interpretation from the text receives more attention because the text is more complex. Children are developing strategies that are used to interpret text of various genre. Children are writing well-developed pieces and trying on other author styles and genres.

Fluency 3 Behaviors of Reading and Writing

Reading	*Writing*
Uses own experiences to understand interpretation of author's message.	Conventional spelling is utilized most often with inventive spelling used for unfamiliar words.
While reading can understand most figurative language and humor by explaining meaning.	Can develop at least 2 areas (beginning, middle, end) in writing.
Can understand there are different viewpoints of interpretation of text.	Attempting to write on specific aspect of topic with supporting details.
Can identify problem/resolution and cause/effect in reading.	Uses a variety of simple sentences with dependent clauses.
Can write a summary of the plot by stating beginning, middle, and end of story.	Able to copy authors' styles in writing.
Can identify multi-dimensional characters and state multi-attributes.	Attempting to write in different forms or genres.
Can identify setting and climax of story.	Uses some character development in writing.
Can identify general genre areas: realistic fiction, fantasy (magical), poetry, traditional literature, and nonfiction in reading books.	

Focus Areas for Fluency 3 Level

1. Can identify the literary elements of title, author, major characters, minor characters, summary of plot, setting, problem/resolution, climax, and genre or form.

2. Reading from a variety of genre.

3. Responding to books through writing.

4. Writing pieces are reflecting other authors' styles and different genres.

General Instructional Format for Reading (based on 3 - 5 instructional sessions per book)

1. At the Fluency 3 level, the teacher will ask the children to read silently. Teacher will often have students complete silent reading before coming to the group meeting.

2. Children and teacher discuss the meaning of the book from questions about the book. These questions are often given to the students to answer after they have read the book and before coming to the group.

3. Sometimes the teacher can discuss vocabulary words if they are crucial to the understanding of the text and context is not helpful.

4. Teacher selects specific behaviors to work on with children from list depending on abilities of children and book selected. S/he provides reinforcement on these behaviors/strategies using a game, worksheet, or writing task.

5. Teacher selects activities for children to do with book from suggested activities list.

Suggested Activities to Encourage Behaviors at Fluency 3 Level

1. Responding to the text continues to be a focus with emphasis on the use of their own experiences in relationship to the text. That is, the children are encouraged to relate what they read to their own experiences and to other books. The teacher will need to demonstrate and model this responding. The students will need support to do this activity independently at this level.

2. Exposure to various genre is important at this level. A class or group chart of the books read and genre could be developed. The teacher would discuss the characteristics of the genre and list those elements depicted in the book on the chart as well.

3. Setting and climax are introduced and discussed at this level. To assist in this discussion, the teacher and children can construct a line graph of the story's excitement levels which would indicate the climax. For setting, the teacher and children could rewrite a passage in another setting to compare and contrast. Discussing the author intent in using a specific setting would also be helpful.

4. Writing in a particular genre or author's style will be helpful in encouraging understanding of genre and style. A group project will probably be most successful since the children need a lot of support at this level.

Benchmarks of Acquisition for Fluency 3 Level

Reading

1. Able to complete a literary elements chart with some teacher support. The chart includes:

> Title, author
> Major and minor characters

        Summary of plot
        Setting, genre
        Problem/resolution
        Climax

2. Can write a response to the Fluency 3 book read silently and give reasons or support for response from the text.

Writing

3. Writing pieces are cohesive, and use descriptive language and a variety of sentence structures.

4. Attempting to use other styles or forms.

5. Writing pieces show some character development.

Assessment Procedures

1. Children are asked to silently read the story.

2. The children are asked to complete a chart which contains the literary elements.

3. The teacher asks the students to respond to the book and give reasons.

4. From various writing pieces the teacher can observe the progress in writing.

Note: If the child has difficulty with only a couple of items, the teacher can use her/his judgement in deciding whether the child is ready for the challenges at the next level. The teacher can note any failed items on the Benchmark Record

Keeping Chart (see Appendix) and continues to work on them in the next level. The teacher can retest on those items when the child has demonstrated knowledge.

FLUENCY 4 LEVEL

Fluency 4 Level refines the previous Fluency 3 level strategies and genre study. All types of text are read and the literary elements are known and applied in writing. The children develop the ability to integrate the text and their own experiences in responding to literature. Writing pieces are well developed and interesting. The writing communicates a clear message.

Fluency 4 Behaviors of Reading and Writing

Reading

Can understand various viewpoints of interpretation of author's message.

Attempting to relate interpretation of author's message to another text already read.

Uses own experiences to understand interpretation of author's message and can relate support from experiences to interpretation.

Can identify figurative language/humor and attempts to state author's purpose for use in text.

Can list multi-dimensions of characters and uses text to support attributes.

Can identify setting and shifts in setting.

Able to understand some characteristics of the various genres.

Writing

Able to copy author style or genre form in writing.

Can write to effectively convey message.

Can develop all areas (beginning, middle, end) in writing.

Attempting to paragraph but not using indentations.

Writes on specific aspect of topic with supporting details.

Attempting to write a lead sentence which will interest the reader.

Uses complex sentences.

Focus Areas for Fluency 4 Level

1. Reading and understanding of various genre characteristics.

2. Vocabulary development, sentence structure, organization of text, and understanding in all genres.

3. Responding to literature by integrating own experiences and text.

4. Writing to communicate a message.

General Instructional Format for Reading (based on 3 - 5 instructional sessions per book)

1. At the Fluency 4 level, the teacher will ask the children to read silently. The teacher will have students complete silent reading before coming to the group meeting.

2. Children and teacher discuss the meaning of the book from questions about the book. These questions are given to the students to answer after they have read the book and before coming to the group.

3. Sometimes the teacher can discuss vocabulary words if they are crucial to the understanding of the text and context is not helpful.

4. The teacher selects specific behaviors to work on with children from list depending on abilities of children and book selected. S/he provides reinforcement on these behaviors/strategies using a game, worksheet, or writing task.

5. The teacher selects activities for children to do with the book from suggested activities list.

Suggested Activities to Encourage Behaviors at Fluency 4 Level

1. Reading and understanding of all types of books including textbooks are focused on at this level. Pace, purpose, genre, and complexity are characteristics that influence the reader. These areas as well as study skills can be developed.

2. More in-depth study of genre can be presented and supported by the teacher. A literature theme such as poetry or mysteries can be developed over a period of time. This theme study can also develop point of view and characteristics of various genre.

3. The teacher can direct frequent responding to books read. Students will begin to develop the ability to respond personally with support and relate the text to another book read or experiences in their own lives. Teachers could encourage this type of response by asking the question: What part of the book read reminds you of something in your own life or reminds you of another book read? Students can keep logs of these entries.

4. Nonfiction is emphasized at this level. A group project might be to select a general topic like the ocean, which has fiction and nonfiction available. The students begin reading nonfiction material about the ocean. After several demonstrations by the teacher, the students are asked to write down facts learned from the nonfiction material without the books. These notes would be used to write a group fiction story on the ocean incorporating facts into the fiction. Some students might be encouraged to try this activity on their own.

Benchmarks of Acquisition for Fluency 4 Level

Reading

1. Can list 3 statements of fact learned from a nonfiction selection.

2. Understands a nonfiction selection and can use selection to create a journal entry that integrates the selection and student's experiences.

3. Can independently complete a literary elements chart.

Writing

4. Writing pieces are well developed and indicate some use of other styles and forms.

5. Writing pieces are interesting and present a clear image to the reader.

Assessment Procedures

1. Children are asked to silently read the story.

2. The children are asked to list 3 facts learned from the book.

3. The teacher asks the students to respond to the book by creating a journal entry that utilizes both inference and own experience.

4. The teacher asks the students to complete a literary elements chart on an independent reading book.

5. From various writing pieces, the teacher can observe the progress in writing.

Note: If the child has difficulty with only a couple of items, the teacher can use her/his judgement in deciding whether the child is ready for the challenges at the next level. The teacher can note any failed items on the Benchmark Record Keeping Chart (see Appendix) and continues to work on them in the next level. The teacher can retest on those items when the child has demonstrated knowledge.

Summary

This chapter discussed the Fluency Literacy Levels. The key areas for these levels are:

Key Reading Areas

Fluency 1 (F 1)

-Begins to take an active role in interacting
with author
-Responds to/shares reading experiences
-Cueing strategies are automatic

Fluency 2 (F 2)

-Active role in interacting with author
-Begins to make interpretations about text
-Uses own experiences to respond to text
-Cueing strategies are automatic

Fluency 3 (F 3)

-Engaged with author
-Interprets text using experiences
-Reads for meaning and to learn from text
-Sharing/responding to text using experiences

Fluency 4 (F 4)

-Reads many different styles, authors, forms
-Interprets text using experiences
-Reads for meaning and to learn from text
-Independently reads, responds, and shares

Key Writing Areas

Fluency 1 (F 1)

> -Able to write on a topic and maintain focus
> -Story has a beginning, middle, and end
> -Uses a variety of simple sentence structures

Fluency 2 (F 2)

> -Becoming more detailed in writing
> -Uses descriptive language in writing
> -Conventional spelling is dominant

Fluency 3 (F 3)

> -Beginning to expand into different forms of writing
> -More development can be seen in the beginning, middle,
> and end of writing
> -Uses more complex sentence structure

Fluency 4 (F 4)

> -Beginning, middle, and end of story is well developed
> -Can support writing with details
> -Can imitate an author or genre
> -Uses complex sentences

Chapter 13   Literacy Beyond the Fluency Levels

Children who have acquired the competencies in the literacy levels are well on their way to becoming independent readers and writers. They have learned how to read, and the focus shifts to reading to learn. That is not to say that they have not learned anything from reading up to this point, but, rather, the emphasis in strategy instruction has shifted from breaking the code to more complex understandings of the text.

The reading to learn strategies are beyond the scope of this book. However, the main areas of study will be described for teachers. These areas are literary elements, organizational patterns of text, and independent reading and writing.

As a result of the acquisition of the competencies of the literacy levels, the literary elements can be identified by students and have been discussed in detail. Beyond Fluency 4, the text material read by students becomes increasingly more complex. This requires in-depth study in the literary elements. Let's briefly look at each of these elements.

Characterization becomes more difficult with the introduction of complex characters. Characters are multi-dimensional and change over time in the books. The students are encouraged to give depth to their characters in writing pieces. The styles authors use in developing characters, such as character reaction to events, are studied at length.

Plots and their settings are becoming more complex in that there are subplots and multiple settings in a book. The use of subplots to develop a book and the use of setting changes to create moods are important to understanding an author's message. These study areas require the use of critical thinking skills and interpretation.

The climax of a story in the early and most fluency level books usually came at one specific point in the plot. Now, in books beyond fluency, there may be several climaxes. The instruction focuses on determining the influence and significance of these climaxes on the author's message.

Understanding these literary elements in depth will assist the student in the interpretation of text and in developing his/her own style of writing.

The organizational patterns of text: cause/effect, comparison/contrast, problem/resolution, concept by examples, description, and sequence as discussed by Jones, Palincsar, Ogle, and Carr (1987) can be crucial to understanding text. These authors support the concept that students who can identify and understand these patterns in text are better able to understand the message. Likewise, in writing, the knowledge of these organizational patterns can assist the student in clear communication of his/her message. The organizational pattern of writing can influence the reader's understanding of that writing.

Beyond Fluency 4, independent reading and writing is fostered to a large extent. Since the students are able to read and write with minimal teacher support, then the strategies and behaviors of independent reading and writing become paramount. Classroom practice reflects this focus with more time for independent reading and writing.

Development of these reading to learn strategies continues through the whole language components and learning aspects of model/demonstration, interaction, support, and independence. However, they tend to look different in classroom practice. The Independent Reading and Independent Writing components tend to get more time in the classroom. Shared Reading uses chapter books frequently. Therefore, the class might use one book for several weeks. Guided Reading moves from predominately literacy level grouping to skill or focus groupings. These groups may change from day to day. This Guided Reading will more often focus on interpretation of the Shared Book or Independent Reading book. Read To continues, but the purpose is less of modeling the act of reading and more in exposing students to different forms of literature to influence independent reading.

Guided Writing will take the form of projects that last for several weeks. The projects would include various units of study such as poetry, where several different forms and styles are presented to the students. Students select the form and style to try in their own piece of writing.

Independent Writing also has a major focus. Besides providing more classroom time for Independent Writing, specific strategies for independence in writing are developed through mini-lessons and conferencing.

In terms of the learning aspects (model/demonstration, interaction, support, and independence), all are included in each experience as before in learning to read. However, the emphasis shifts to independence. The teacher might use a mini lesson for the modeling and conferencing to lend support. The students will interact with the text and/or writing piece for understanding. However, encouraging and promoting independence is the primary focus.

In conclusion, the whole language components change in structure but are vital to literacy development beyond Fluency 4. Moreover, the learning aspects continue to foster growth in literacy beyond Fluency 4.

Summary

1. Literacy beyond Fluency 4 is characteristic of reading to learn and independent learning.

2. Teachers will need to change the emphasis of the whole language components to fit the changing needs of students. However, the basic concepts developed in each component continue to be important in literacy development beyond Fluency 4.

Chapter 14   Assessing the Literacy Level Needs of Your Students

In this chapter, assessing the needs of students in terms of the literacy levels will be discussed. The class as well as individual students require assessment in terms of the literacy levels to ensure appropriate learning experiences.

The whole language teacher is responsible for assessing her/his students and determining what types of strategies and skills need encouragement to progress in learning to read and write. The teacher can begin by dividing her/his class into three groups of above-average, average, and below-average students. For each group, it is important to determine the students' abilities to segment the language, understand the text, apply cueing strategies in oral reading, and write a story. The teacher could ask them all to complete these tasks and then go to a specific benchmark literacy level.

Segmentation of words and syllables, but not sounds, indicates that the child can try an Early 1 or 2 level for understanding. If all segmentation areas are in place, then the child can try the Early 3 or higher level for understanding. The application of cueing strategies in oral reading can be helpful in determining which of these levels to try. The teacher can also ask the students to write on one topic for a limited period of time to assess their writing progress.

Since individual benchmarking can be time consuming, trying to pinpoint an approximate level is helpful. For the average group, the teacher can refer to the "Literacy Level Chart and Whole Language Components" found in Chapter 9 to find the literacy level expected for these children and try benchmarking at this level. For the high and below groups, the teacher can go higher or lower than the expectation for her/his grade level children.

Some other general guidelines for reading would include using the four major stages of reading development — pre-emergent, emergent, early, and fluency — to determine the general stage area of the student. If one thinks of these stages in general terms, then an emergent reader is a child who has developed a love for books, enjoys having books read to him/her, and listens attentively but is not able to use pictures to glean elements of the message. If the child does not have these behaviors, then s/he is probably pre-emergent.

The early reader is one who can follow the print as a teacher reads and perhaps knows some words in isolation, but basically needs to be taught the cueing and meaning strategies useful for reading. The cueing strategies include picture clues, word order clues (syntax), meaning clues (semantics), and sound/symbol clues (phonics). The reader at the fluency stage, on the other hand, has knowledge of all the cueing strategies, is developing sight vocabulary rapidly, and is ready for higher level thinking skills in comprehension. There are four levels in each of the early and fluency stages, which gives the teacher a broad range of competencies to consider in assessing instructional needs.

In writing, we can generally use the same stages as guidelines. The pre-emergent writer uses pictures to convey his/her message. The emergent writer is using pictures and attempting to write some letters or a word. At the early stage of writing, the student moves from writing letters to represent words to writing simple sentences using inventive and conventional spelling. Writing pieces with a beginning, middle, and end becomes the focus of a writer at the fluency stage. Also, the fluent writer tries to imitate different authors and genres in communicating his/her message.

Once the literacy level has been narrowed to a couple of levels, then the teacher can assess each benchmark associated with that level. To standardize this assessment for all children the teacher may want to develop a benchmark kit.

To develop a benchmark kit the teacher needs to select books not read by students from each of the literacy levels. Next, s/he needs to develop assessment activities using the book to assess all benchmarks listed under a level. These books and activities can be put in a box or file for easy access as the benchmark kit.

Moreover, as the children begin to demonstrate the reading/writing behaviors at a specific literacy level, then the benchmark kit can be used to assess progress. Using this kit the teacher can make judgements as to when children require further challenging in more difficult text.

In addition, the teacher will want to understand the literacy needs of her/his students as a class in order to provide appropriate learning experiences in Shared Reading and Guided Writing. Both of these components involve whole class projects. After the individual literacy needs of the students have been determined, then the teacher can determine where the majority of students have needs and can develop projects for Shared Reading and Guided Writing based on these findings. The "Literacy Level Chart and Whole Language Components" found in Chapter 9 may be useful in this assessment. This chart shows where you might typically find most of your students at a given grade level or the average for that grade level.

Summary

1. In order to determine the literacy level of your student, one must first generally assess the student's competencies in terms of the stages of pre-emergent, emergent, early, and fluency.

2. Developing a benchmark kit can help to standardize the assessment of your students.

3. Providing activities that require the benchmark behaviors will assess the specific literacy level of your students.

4. For Shared Reading and Guided Writing, assessing the average abilities of your students is helpful.

Chapter 15   Determining the Literacy Level of Your Literature

The traditional system of leveling books used a readability formula that took into consideration the number of words per sentence, number of sentences and perhaps syllables. Since the basal reader was developed using the number of words and length of sentences, this grading system worked well. However, in whole language we want to encourage the children to take on the role of the reader from the beginning by reading whole books. Since most beginning readers have not acquired all the cueing and meaning strategies necessary to allow them to read with fluency, the literature selected has to support this learning process without becoming frustrating to the student. Therefore, the leveling system has to support and challenge the children in learning to read.

The New Zealand program developed a series called Ready to Read (1984). This series is leveled according to the stages of emergent, early, and fluency. Within the stages of early and fluency, there are four levels. The teachers use their resource guide called Reading in Junior Classes for explanation of the stages and as a guide to instruction. The literacy levels described in this book utilized both of these for their development. The literacy levels were adapted from the New Zealand program in order to fit the American culture.

In the New Zealand program, these books were selected from manuscripts that fulfilled the criteria to be supportive in teaching reading. We have been able to get some of these New Zealand books here in the United States to use but many are culturally biased. In trying to use our own American literature, the task is not easy. Most American literature was written for adults to read aloud to children, as an art form, to retell stories, etc. Most literature was not written exclusively to be read by children. Therefore, one has to be careful to select the literature that will enhance and expand the reading ability of the students without overwhelming them in the beginning stages of learning to read. The New Zealand series appropriately does this in several ways.

First of all the New Zealand series uses interesting, motivating stories. These stories or commentaries are appropriate topics for elementary children and entice them to read. The books are written in large print, except for the late fluency levels, so that children can visually distinguish the words with ease. The language used in the books is familiar to the children because it is in their spoken or listening vocabulary.

Repetition is used in the lower levels to help support the beginning reader. If the kernel sentence is repeated over and over again, then the beginning reader will most likely be able to remember the story as s/he reads along and understand the message of the author. Moreover, the pictures in the books either help to tell the story or enhance the meaning of the text.

The message of the author is delivered mostly in the pictures in the lower levels and then exclusively in the text in the late fluency levels. The books support the children in the early stage as they acquire the strategies of context and sound/symbol association in reading to understand the message. In the fluency stage, when the cueing strategies are automatic, the books support the children into further interpretation of the text and learning from the text.

It is only necessary to determine the literacy level of a book when you want to use it for children to learn to read or practice reading. Otherwise, the book is selected for another purpose like demonstrating the characteristics of a tall tale or illustrating figurative language. In these cases, the readability of the text for the students is secondary to this purpose.

Your first consideration in leveling your literature is to identify your primary purpose in using the book. If your purpose is to assist children in learning to read, then you can proceed to level the book. If your primary purpose is different, then leveling the book may not be necessary. Some books are not appropriate for children to use for learning to read because the format and language is not conducive to what the children are capable of handling at this time. However, it does not mean that the book is of no value to children. It only means that it will not be helpful for them in using the book to learn to read. It will probably be an excellent book to have read aloud, shared by the teacher, or for them to "read" the pictures.

When you have established your primary purpose for using the book to assist children in learning to read, then you need to consider the following aspects to determine if the book is appropriate for leveling. All of these characteristics need to be present in order to follow the leveling procedure. If the following characteristics are not all present, then turn to the Imbalance Literature section for further analysis of the book.

Characteristics Necessary for Leveling Procedure

1. The story must be motivating, exciting, and interesting to young children. It is a story worth reading.

2. The story plot or concept must be relatively simple for young children. At the end of the fluency levels, the plot becomes somewhat more complex but still appropriate for young children.

3. The sentence structure in the book must be simple to moderately complex. An example of a simple sentence is: Terry likes to eat oranges. An example of a complex sentence is: After the school play, Tom and his friends went downtown to the ice cream shop to purchase ice cream cones.

4. The language used in the text must be familiar to young children. The vocabulary used is part of young children's spoken language and listening language. If technical or more obscure language is used, then the pictures or text define it.

5. The pictures in the book are important. At the lower levels of emergent and early, they help to tell the story. At emergent, the pictures and text have a one-to-one match. The pictures tell the story. As the levels increase, the role of pictures diminishes to enhancing the text.

Leveling Procedure

First of all, be sure the book has all of the necessary characteristics by reading the book. After it has been read in its entirety, answer the following questions to determine its literacy level. It is important to keep in mind that leveling books is subjective. It is helpful to have books already leveled to use as examples for each level as you try to level a new book. Here are some general guidelines, but teacher judgement in leveling books is most important.

1. Is the book's cover, title, and format appropriate for elementary age children to use in learning to read?

>   Yes - Go to question 2
>   No - Go to Imbalanced Literature section

2. Does the book communicate an appropriate message for elementary age children?

>   Yes - Go to question 3
>   No - Go to Imbalanced Literature section

3. Does the book have several pages (more than 2 pages) of full-page print?

>   Yes - Go to question 9
>   No - Go to question 4

4. Does the book have small print as if a business typewriter was used?

>   Yes - Go to Imbalanced Literature section
>   No - Go to question 5

5. Does the book have one, two, three, or four lines of print per page but only 1-3 sentences and/or a combination (some pages have one line, others three lines, and still others have two lines, etc.) ?

>   Yes - You have an Em, E 1, or E 2 book.
>   Go to question 6
>   No - Go to question 7

6. Read the following descriptions of the characteristics of the level. Select the book level that most closely fits the characteristics.

Emergent Book (Em)

- pictures and text agree on a one-to-one basis, that is, what is written is pictured in the book
-there is usually less than one, one, or two lines of print
-the same basic sentence or phrase is repeated on page after page with one-word or two-word changes from page to page
-the word changes are pictured on the page
-the word changes are usually at the beginning or end of the sentence
-vocabulary and sentence structure are simple

Early 1 (E 1)

- pictures and text agree on a one-to-one basis, that is, what is written is pictured in the book
-there is usually one or two lines of print
-the same basic sentence or phrase is repeated on page after page with word changes
-the word changes are pictured on the page
-the word changes are often embedded in the *sentence*
-vocabulary and sentence structure are simple

Early 2 (E 2)

- pictures and text agree
-there is usually more than one line of print but not more than four lines
-repetition is still prevalent but there are often two phrases or kernel sentences repeated
-the word changes can be in any position of the sentence
-vocabulary and sentence structure are simple

7. Does each page of the book have 2-6 lines of print with 2-4 or more sentences? There are no more than 2 full pages of print in the book.

> Yes - You have and E 3 or E 4 book. Go on
> to question 8
> No - Go back to question 3

8. Read the following descriptions of the characteristics of the level. Select the book level which most closely fits the characteristics.

> Early 3 (E 3)
>
>> -there can be some repetition from page to page but the unit of repetition is usually larger than one sentence
>> -pictures support the meaning of the text but more meaning is in the text
>> -the average page length is 4 lines
>> -vocabulary and sentence structure are simple
>
> Early 4 (E 4)
>
>> -there is usually no repetition
>> -pictures support the meaning of the text but more meaning is in the text
>> -the average page length is 5-6 lines
>> -vocabulary and sentence structure are simple but sentences are becoming more complex

9. In reading the book, will the child mostly get meaning from the text and a little from the pictures?

> Yes - You have a Fluency book. Go to
> question 10
> No - Go to Imbalanced Literature section

10. Is the readability of the text not greater than a 3.0 grade level as designated by the publisher or as determined through the use of a readability formula? (Note: If the text readability level is unavailable, you must make a subjective judgement call by skimming the text to determine if the story line is appropriate through grade 3. If it is beyond an average third grader's typical reading material, then it does not fit these levels.)

> Yes - Go to question 11
> No - This book does not fit these levels.

11. Is the print larger than this (walk to the store) on the pages of the book?

> Yes - Go to question 12
> No - Go to Imbalanced Literature section

12. Does the book have specialized vocabulary that would require extraordinary experiential background to understand?

> Yes - Go to Imbalanced Literature section
> No - Go to question 13

13. Does the book require frequent interpretation or require inferential thinking throughout, that is, on most pages there is figurative language or inference?

> Yes - You have a F 3 or F 4 book. Go to question 16
> No - Go to question 14

14. Does the book require occasional interpretation, maybe once or twice in the book?

> Yes - You have a Fluency 2 book.
> No - Go to question 15

15. Is the book basically at the literal level of understanding, that is, what is written is what happened?

> Yes - You have a Fluency 1 book.
> No - Go to Imbalanced Literature section

16. Read the following descriptions of the characteristics of the level. Select the book level that most closely fits the characteristics.

Fluency 3 (F 3)

> -pictures enhance the text but lend little support to meaning of the text
> -meaning is beyond the print
> -sentence structures are complex and varied
> -there is a variety of genre, nonfiction has a significant focus
> -plots are well developed
> -usually is a chapter book

Fluency 4 (F 4)

> -a few pictures which enhance the text
> -meaning is beyond the print
> -sentence structures are complex and varied
> -there is a variety of genre, nonfiction has a significant focus
> -plots are well developed
> -most often is a chapter book
> -vocabulary is usually more difficult than Fluency 3
> -format of book requires more interpretation for meaning

Imbalance Literature

If you have been referred to this section, then the book you read does not fit all the criteria for a specific literacy level. Now it is important to look more critically at the book.

Your best choice in the case of imbalanced literature is to try it out on some children who you know are at a specific literacy level. Do they like the book? With assistance from you, can they read and understand the book? Would they like to read it?

Your second choice is to read it to children and enjoy it that way. Some books are just better being read aloud rather than being read by children.

Lastly, here are some questions to consider as a guide in trying to determine the literacy level.

1. Does the book have small print, difficult vocabulary, and complex sentences but the age level and appeal of the book is for young children? Then perhaps this book would be better as a book one reads to children. If the text is so difficult that it would qualify for Fluency 3 or 4, then ask yourself if a third grader would select it for reading. If not, it is better as a read aloud.

2. Sometimes there is only one or two sentences per page but the sentence is complex, the vocabulary is difficult, and there is no repetition. If this is the case, then the book will generally have to start as a Fluency 1 book because the children will need to have the cueing strategies in place in order to read and understand the text. Will second graders enjoy this book or is it best as a read aloud?

3. Often there is print in several locations on a page. This layout makes it difficult to read and you would need to begin at a Fluency 1 level. The appropriate level would depend on how much interpretation is needed and difficult vocabulary is present.

4. Nonfiction books tend to require competencies at Fluency 3 and Fluency 4. However, pictures should be present on each page to lend support in

reading. The specialized vocabulary in a nonfiction book makes it difficult to read and understand.

In conclusion, the leveling of books is not a science but rather an art form. As beauty is in the eye of the beholder, imbalanced literature placement is in the mind of the reader.

Summary

The following figure briefly describes the basic reading aspects of each literacy level. This black and white chart is a guide for the role each leveled book can play in reading development. A similar color coded chart can be found towards the end of this book.

Defining Literacy Levels for Whole Language

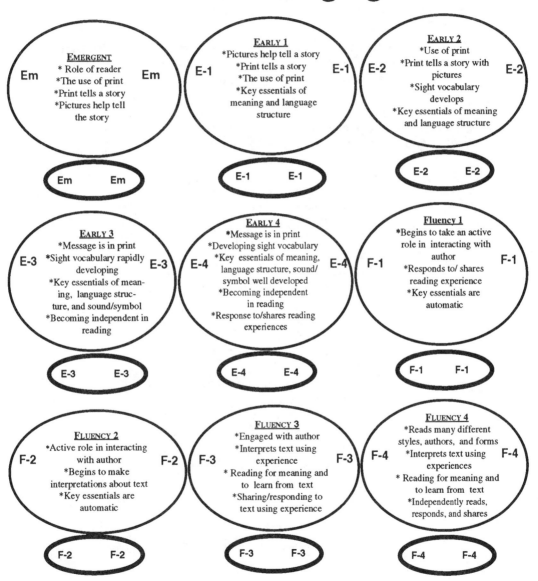

EMERGENT
* Role of reader
*The use of print
*Print tells a story
*Pictures help tell the story

Em   Em   Em   Em

EARLY 1
*Pictures help tell a story
*Print tells a story
*The use of print
*Key essentials of meaning and language structure

E-1   E-1   E-1   E-1

EARLY 2
*Use of print
*Print tells a story with pictures
*Sight vocabulary develops
*Key essentials of meaning and language structure

E-2   E-2   E-2   E-2

EARLY 3
*Message is in print
*Sight vocabulary rapidly developing
*Key essentials of meaning, language structure, and sound/symbol
*Becoming independent in reading

E-3   E-3   E-3   E-3

EARLY 4
*Message is in print
*Developing sight vocabulary
*Key essentials of meaning, language structure, sound/symbol well developed
*Becoming independent in reading
*Response to/shares reading experiences

E-4   E-4   E-4   E-4

Fluency 1
*Begins to take an active role in interacting with author
*Responds to/ shares reading experience
*Key essentials are automatic

F-1   F-1   F-1   F-1

FLUENCY 2
*Active role in interacting with author
*Begins to make interpretations about text
*Key essentials are automatic

F-2   F-2   F-2   F-2

FLUENCY 3
*Engaged with author
*Interprets text using experience
* Reading for meaning and to learn from text
*Sharing/responding to text using experience

F-3   F-3   F-3   F-3

FLUENCY 4
*Reads many different styles, authors, and forms
*Interprets text using experiences
* Reading for meaning and to learn from text
*Independently reads, responds, and shares

F-4   F-4   F-4   F-4

*An improved adaptation for literature leveling devised by **Brenda M. Weaver** Language Arts Coordinator*

Published by *Story House Corp.*, Charlotteville, NY 12036 Copyright © 1992 by STORY HOUSE CORP:

Chapter 16 A Typical Day in a Whole Language Classroom

There seem to be two confusing areas for teachers as they begin to implement whole language. One area is how much time is spent in each component and the other is what all of the components look like in a typical day.

The amount of time spent in each component depends on the development of the class. The components are meant to be used to promote literacy learning and fit the needs of your students. Here are some general guidelines based on what an average grade level student demonstrates as his/her needs.

Kindergarten	Read To- daily, 10-15 minutes
	Shared Reading/Language Experience -
	    if a full-day kindergarten, then daily;
	    if a half-day kindergarten, then about
	    three times per week
	Writing-as often as time allows, often
	    related to theme and/or Shared Reading

Grade 1	Read To-daily, 15 minutes
	Shared Reading/Language Experience - daily,
	    20-30 minutes
	Guided Reading - daily, 45-60 minutes;
	    depends on number of groups, about
	    15 minutes per group
	Guided Writing - about 3 times per week,
	    often a follow-up to Shared Reading
	Independent Reading - children find this
	    difficult to sustain for long periods of time,
	    usually an option during independent work
	    time
	Independent Writing - Children write journals
	    and stories during independent work time

Grade 2   Read To - daily, 15 minutes
Shared Reading - daily, approx. 30-40 minutes
Guided Reading - daily, 45-60 minutes;
   depends on number of groups,
   15-20 minutes per group
Guided Writing - 3-4 times per week, often a
   follow-up to shared reading
Independent Reading - 2-3 times per week,
   part of independent work time as well
Independent Writing - 2-3 times per week
   opposite Independent Reading, also a part
   of independent work time

Grade 3   Read To - daily, 15 minutes
Shared Reading - daily, approx. 20-30 minutes
Guided Reading - daily, 45-60 minutes; depends
   on number of groups, 15-20 minutes per
   group
Guided Writing - 3-4 times per week, often a
   follow-up to Shared Reading
Independent Reading - 2-3 times per week,
   part of independent work time as well
Independent Writing - 2-3 times per week
   opposite Independent Reading, also a part
   of independent work time

Here is an example of a teacher's lesson plans for a day using the whole language approach and literacy levels for **second grade**.

9 - 9:10   Attendance and lunch count

9:10 - 9:40   **Shared Reading**

Class set of *Imogene's Antlers* by David Small
(New York: Crown Publishers, Inc., 1985)

Purposes: Read together to establish problem/
resolution of story and discuss plot. Reinforce use
of cueing strategies with 4 vocabulary words:
consulted, advice, milliner, disappeared.

Follow-up activity: Students summarize main
events in story and illustrate each event. After
the last event the children will write their own
reason for why Imogene grew antlers. These
reasons will be discussed tomorrow.

9:40 - 10:40   **Guided Reading:** 4 groups in classroom: E 2, E 3,
E 4, and F 1. Each group is instructed for 15 min-
utes

E 2 Book: *Nicky Upstairs and Down* by Harriet
Ziefert, pictures by Richard Brown (New York:
Penguin, 1987)

Purposes: The teacher and children will read the book together for meaning and understanding. Children will reread the
book together for fluency. The teacher will give a word on an
index card to find in the book. After the children find the
word, they will tell the teacher how many sounds they hear
in the word. This exercise is repeated so each student has a
chance to respond (segmentation of sounds).

Follow-up activity: Choose a partner and read book
to him/her.

E 3 Book: *Stitches* by Harriet Ziefert, pictures by Amy Aitken (New York: Penguin, 1990)

Purposes: In previous session, the teacher and children have read and discussed meaning of story. Children take turns orally rereading to practice cueing strategies. As a group, with the teacher writing, they develop a summary of the book emphasizing beginning, middle, and end of story.

Follow-up activity: Children are asked to write a short story about themselves or someone they know who has had stitches. The teacher reminds them to focus on a beginning, middle, and end in their story.

E 4 Book: *More Spaghetti, I Say!* by Rita Golden Gelman, pictures by Jack Kent (New York: Scholastic, 1977)

Purposes: Children have already read the book and discussed its meaning with the teacher in a previous session. The teacher presents several word cards with words containing the vowel combinations of "ea, ee," some from the book and others not in the book. The teacher assists the children in decoding the words.

Follow-up activity: Students are to complete a cloze activity sheet with sentences that have words containing this vowel combination as well as others studied in previous lessons.

F 1 Book: *I Never Win!* by Judy Delton, pictures by Cathy Gilchrist (New York: Dell, 1981)

Purposes: Students have come to the group

having read the book to themselves. The teacher
and students complete a literary elements chart
of the book which includes author, illustrator,
title, characters, plot, problem/resolution, climax,
and type (genre) as they discuss the meaning of
the book.

Follow-up activity: Children are asked to respond to this book
by writing in their journals what they thought of the book
and relating it to their own experiences. These responses will
be shared in the next session.

All follow-up activities are reviewed by the teacher the following day in
Guided Reading.

During Guided Reading, children not meeting with the teacher can do
the following independent work: journal writing, spelling study, follow-up to
Shared and Guided Reading, **Independent Reading, Independent Writing**,
and instructional games.

10:40 - 11:10	Music Class

11:10 - 11:40   **Guided Writing**
Purposes: After reviewing the problem/resolution
of the Shared Reading book, the teacher asks the
children for their ideas as to what might have
happened if the problem was not resolved in this
way. What other ways could the story have
been resolved? What are the results of the
problem being solved in these new ways?
The children write the alternative ending of the
book. As the children are writing, the teacher
moves around the room to assist various children.

11:40 - 12:15   Math

12:15 - 12:45	Lunch
12:45 - 1:10	**Read To**
1:10 - 1:40	Gym Class
1:40 - 2:10	Science or Health
2:10 - 2:40	Social Studies
2:40 - 3:10	Independent Writing on self-selected topics. Mini lesson: Writing sentences complete with punctuation and capitalization. Teacher confers with several students as well.

This daily plan is only one example of how these components are used to teach the language arts. Each day the classroom of a whole language teacher is different and therefore s/he must use flexible scheduling and grouping. It should also be noted that on some days the teacher may group heterogeneously not according to literacy levels but rather for a specific purpose. These groups are flexible and constantly changing. It is not the structured group set-up like the basal. The teacher uses flexible grouping because children develop at different paces, and certain children require more practice and reinforcement than others.

Both of these sets of guidelines are meant to give the transitioning teacher some examples as to what a typical day might look like. As teachers become more familiar with the components, they begin to integrate the content areas into all of the components. For example, a teacher might use literature for Shared Reading that is on a social studies or science topic. Therefore, in the discussion the class would discuss the content topic and reading strategies for understanding this book. In Guided Writing, the class project might be to write a nonfiction class book on the content topic.

In general, the components and time guidelines are flexible to meet the needs of the children involved. The primary purpose for having components and monitoring their use in a classroom is to ensure that all aspects of learning are experienced by the children, and that children progress in learning to read and write.

Summary

1. For the teacher who is transitioning into whole language, time spent on the whole language components is important. Monitoring the use of these components is important in providing a balanced whole language program that promotes growth in literacy development.

2. While general guidelines can be given for time spent on each whole language component, the teacher's judgement of the needs of her/his class and the type of learning experiences provided are important to the allocation of classroom time.

3. There is no "typical" day in the classroom of a whole language teacher. However, an example of how a beginning whole language teacher might allocate her/his time is provided.

4. As the teacher becomes experienced with the whole language components, integration with the content area subjects takes place. The goal in whole language is to integrate all subjects throughout the school day.

Chapter 17 Assessment in the Whole Language Classroom

Whole language is a process curriculum or a curriculum that requires gradual development and is ever changing. Collaborative development of whole language curriculum seems to develop ownership by the teachers and administrators in this curriculum. So, too, with assessment collaboration is vital to the success of the assessment guidelines.

Sometimes whole language teachers can neglect assessment in their programs because of the overwhelming interest in using literature and developing writing. Assessment needs to be examined and established right along with the whole language curriculum so that monitoring can occur.

Since process curriculums utilize different strategies and skills in learning than the product curriculums, the meaning of success in terms of student achievement must be redefined. In the traditional system, the paper was given a numerical grade. In a process curriculum like whole language, a grade does not tell the whole story. It does not express how the student moved from a jumble of words to a cohesive story in the piece of writing or how responding to literature required that the student use the book and his/her own experiences to relate to the piece of literature. Whole language as a process curriculum requires different assessments. Let's look at some of these assessments and how they can be utilized in the classroom.

First of all, each whole language component requires assessment in terms of its purpose in the development of literacy. For the Read To component, the central focus is listening skills and enjoyment of literature. Here are some questions the teacher might want to include in an observational checklist:

1. Does the student listen attentively to the read aloud?

2. Does the student listen attentively to others when they share information or ask questions?

3. Does the student comprehend the read aloud?

4. Is the student able to remember from day to day what is happening in the read aloud chapter book?

5. Can the student compare and contrast various read alouds?

In Shared Reading, the teacher will want to assess various areas. If the Shared Reading book is close to the reading ability of the student, then the teacher can assess the oral and silent reading strategies. The teacher can have the student orally read a passage from the book. The teacher writes down what is read by the student and compares errors or miscues. This running record can be helpful in looking at the student's ability to apply cueing strategies. For silent reading, the teacher can ask, orally or in written form, questions about the book for understanding. Since the follow-up activity usually reinforces the teacher's purposes for sharing this literature, it can be used as an assessment tool on a daily basis.

The benchmarks of the various literacy levels can be used for assessment in the Guided Reading component. Guided Reading groups are often based on literacy level and the benchmarks can be effective tools for assessment. Some teachers report to parents the progress of their child in terms of the literacy levels because the benchmarks provide somewhat of a standard measuring stick for all children.

For Independent Reading, the student usually keeps a reading response log. As the child reads books, s/he writes a response to this book in his/her log. The teacher can evaluate this log on a continuum. First of all, the child will often respond by summarizing the book in some manner. This type of response is at the low end of the continuum. Later, the child will often respond by interpreting what happened in the book based on his/her own experiences. The highest level of response is when the child responds by demonstrating understanding and interpretation of the book and relating this book to his/her own experiences. For example, the student might respond to a book by explaining that this book reminds him/her of the time that his/her family went to Florida. The student continues to relate the events and feelings in the book to this real-life experience. For very young children, a brief summary of the book can be a big accomplishment.

Moreover, during student-teacher conferences on the book being read, the teacher can ask questions, ask the child to support his/her position from passages in the text, and record the strategies and skills the child has demonstrated. Teachers often have the children keep working folders for Independent Reading for the purpose of keeping this information together.

Guided Writing usually involves a class project in writing. For example, all children are going to write their own mysteries. For this component it is suggested that the children and teacher set the standards and requirements for the writing project. In this way everyone has ownership into the assessment. An evaluation sheet can be written and given to all children. At the completion of the project, students and parents as well as the teacher can evaluate the projects.

The conferencing in Independent Writing is a rich source for assessment. As the teacher conferences with the student, s/he can record the skills worked on, the degree to which the child has progressed, and the future objectives of writing for this child. Teachers often have a working writing folder for the child to keep the writing pieces in progress and to record the conference information.

Journal writing is also another avenue for assessment in terms of writing. If children are asked to write in a journal daily, then over time the teacher can observe the progress in writing. S/he can also use the journal writing to assess class needs and provide a mini lesson to boost skills and strategies.

Furthermore, assessment in all of these components will be helpful for the day-to-day learning, but for long-term demonstration of progress a language arts portfolio might be helpful. In this portfolio the teacher can select samples of representative writing throughout the school year. These samples would reflect the steps of the writing process by including rough drafts, revisions, and the final copy. The reading logs and the writing journal inserted into the folder can show progress during the school year as well.

Narratives for both reading and writing can serve to summarize the child's progress over the course of the school year. These narratives can be written a few times during the school year, perhaps the beginning, middle, and end of the school year. In these narratives the teacher would describe the specific strategies, behaviors, and skills the student is demonstrating. S/he would also write about the goals for the student in terms of learning. The literacy levels would be helpful as a guide for the writing of these narratives as well as the conferencing in reading and writing.

Lastly, the Benchmark Record Keeping Chart (see Appendix) and a list of the independent books read by the child might be useful. The teacher receiving all this information the following year would be able to quickly assess the strengths and weaknesses of each student.

All of these assessment records are appropriate and helpful in a whole language program. However, if the school district is requiring standardized testing and numerical grades for the report card then the whole language teacher is in turmoil. It is difficult to blend the two types of assessment. Therefore, from experience, I would recommend that when teachers begin the transition into whole language they also begin to form a committee in the school district that examines the present testing program and report card format. It seems to work best when all of these assessment areas are discussed and changed or modified as whole language is implemented.

Summary

1. Assessment is different in whole language from the traditional program due to the nature of whole language curriculum.

2. Day-to-day assessment can be observed and recorded from the whole language components.

3. Portfolios can provide long-term or school year assessments. These portfolios assist the receiving teacher in making instructional decisions about new students.

Chapter 18 Conclusion

It has been the intent of this book to present some guidelines for teachers as they transition into whole language, and more specifically to define the literacy levels that children progress through on the road to literacy. It has also been the intent of this book to provide a framework or structure for classroom practice in whole language. It is hopeful that this book will benefit all who read it.

Throughout the book references have been made to parental involvement. Parents have a significant role in literacy development. It is beyond the scope of this book to describe in detail all the areas in which parents make a difference, but let's discuss a few activities and programs involving parents.

During the implementing of whole language in either your school or classroom, parents need to be informed and participate where possible. Sometimes the teacher becomes so involved in the learning of whole language methodology that the parental contact can be slighted. This situation can be unfortunate because parents can be strong supporters of the implementation if they are kept informed of the purposes for change and the progress of their children.

Some suggestions and activities that our school has developed include a parent lending library and a parent workshop. In the parent lending library, there are books that can be signed out by parents to read with their children. These books also have activities to be used with the book. Parents often want to help their children and are at a loss as to what to do in terms of whole language curriculum. This library helps to bridge the gap from the old system to the new.

A parent workshop in the evenings was held to inform parents of all the aspects of the whole language program. The literacy levels were discussed. Literature used in the classrooms was shared. Parents experienced a typical day in their child's classroom.

Other parental involvement activities include having the parents' committee of the school sponsor authors, illustrators, and storytellers. Motivational programs include turning off the television and reading and Parents as Reading Partners, where parents and children read together for 15 minutes each night for several weeks.

All of these activities and programs helped to keep the parents informed and involved in the implementation of whole language. Parents are very important to the whole language program.

In summary, I am hopeful that this book has provided the means for teachers to become successful whole language teachers.

Glossary of Terms

Benchmarks for Literacy Levels - Criteria for assessment of student's progress in learning to read and write; competency of these criteria indicates student's readiness for challenges at next literacy level.

Cloze Exercise - A worksheet that usually takes sentences from the text and presents these sentences with words left out; the blanks where the words have been left out are filled in by the students to utilize their abilities in applying the cueing strategies.

Conventions of Print - Aspects of the printed page that need to be understood by the reader in order to grasp the author's message; examples are punctuation, title, author, capitalization, and paragraph indentations.

Cueing Strategies - Strategies that cue or assist the reader in deciphering the words in order to understand the text; picture cues or using pictures in the book, graphophonics or sound/symbol, language structure or syntax, and semantics or meaning are the four strategies discussed in this book.

Genre - Literary form such as fantasy, historical fiction, or picture book.

Guided Reading - A whole language component that involves small group instruction in reading at a literacy level or in a skill/strategy.

Guided Writing - A whole language component that involves instruction in writing directed and supported by the teacher; topics for writing usually focus around a specific genre, author style, or illustrator style.

Independent Reading - A whole language component in which the student selects a book for silent reading; the teacher usually teaches a mini lesson and conferences with students on their reading.

Independent Writing - A whole language component in which the student selects a topic to write about; the teacher usually teaches a mini lesson and conferences with students on their writing.

Language Experience - The teacher writes the story the children dictate; as the teacher writes, s/he demonstrates to the children how spoken language looks in print.

Literary Elements - Those characteristics which define literature, examples: plot, genre, characters, title, etc.

Mini lesson - A five-to-ten minute lesson in which the teacher focuses on one skill or strategy to instruct the children.

Phonemic Awareness - Ability to distinguish the sounds in the language; print is not displayed.

Portfolio - Items selected from a child's work over time to represent his/her progress in literacy development.

Read To - A whole language component in which the teacher reads aloud to the children.

Rewrite - The teacher and students imitate an author by rewriting the story with selected changes such as different characters or a different plot.

Running Record - An assessment device in which the teacher has a student read a passage orally; teacher writes down exactly what the student reads; teacher assesses the reading ability from this recording of the reading.

Segmentation - The ability to distinguish the parts of spoken language or segment the oral language; the parts include words, syllables, and sounds.

Shared Reading - A whole language component in which the children and teacher read together a piece of literature; the teacher provides activities to promote literacy development from this piece of literature.

Appendix

Chart of Literary Elements and the Literacy Levels

Em	Identifies author and illustrator on cover of book.
E 1	Orally can summarize a book.
E 2	Orally can tell the problem/resolution in book read.
E 3	Orally identifies major characters in book. Writes title and author.
E 4	Writes summary of plot. Orally discusses setting and genre.
F 1	Writes characters and attributes. Orally discusses climax.
F 2	Writes summary of plot. Writes problem/resolution.
F 3	Writes all literary elements for book with teacher support.
F 4	Writes all literary elements for book independently.

Chart of Phonics and Structural Analysis Elements for Literacy Levels

Level	Phonics	Structural Analysis
Em	Orally rhyme words	
E 1	Substitute initial Cons. in rhyming	Visual Discrimination of words
	Initial and Final: m, s, b, r, f, t, p, d, n, w, h, l, k, c(s,k), g, g (j), v, y, j, z	Intro to inflectional endings (es,ed,ing,s, est, er, en,'s) and contractions
E 2	Blends and Digraphs: sh, ch, wh, th, th, bl, sp, br, sl, cl, dr, cr, fl, fr, gl, tr, pl, gr, sl, pr, sm, qu, thr, sn, tw, squ, str, sw, sk, spl, sc, spr, scr, shr	Inflectional endings and contractions
E 3	Long and Short Vowels a, e, i, o, u (y) R-controlled or, [er, ir, ur], ar (2 sounds)	Compound words
E 4	oo (2 sounds), [aw, au],	

	ai, ea, oa, ou, ee, ow (2 sounds), ay, ew, [oi, oy], al	re, ex, tion, ious, pre
F 1 **&** **F 2**		in, non, ness, dis, ful, ment, un, ward, able, mis, ish, anti, ist, less, sub, ly

Chart of Four Cueing Strategies of Whole Language

Prerequisite	Type	Level Emphasized	Activities
Able to tell about action in picture	Picture cue	Pre-Em, Em, E 1, E 2; diminished use in E 3, E 4; decorate text, not support in fluency levels	-Use wordless books and have children tell stories -Have children make a story with pictures and tell story
Word segmentation, Syllable segmentation	Semantics (SEM) -meaning Syntax (SYN) -language structure	Em, E 1, E 2; E 3, E 4 - fluency levels becomes automatic	-Develop meaning of unfamiliar words and use in another setting, i.e. write sentences in lang. exper. sent. with unfam. words (SEM) -find unfam. words in other contexts of other books, poems, etc. (SEM) -Take sentences from book or own sent. Put on sent. strips. Cut up words and students put scrambled sent. into approp. order. (SYN) - Compare story read to others with similar meaning (SEM) - Rewrites of books (SEM and SYN) -Students write own stories and teacher

Prerequisite	Type	Level Emphasized	Activities
			conferences w/child in relation to SEM, SYN
Sound segmentation	Sound/symbol	E 3, E 4 Automatic in Fluency Levels	-Sounding out words as writing (invent. spelling) -Select unknown words from book (guided or shared) or use nonsense wds. Decode as a group: a. Can you see any parts you know? b. If yes, divide word into parts by underline and slash. c. Ask students sounds of letters or groups of letters using phonic gen. After establishing what sounds a letter/group could make, ask students which sounds to try d. Instruct in phonic gen. e. Slowly together make sounds in word in order. f. Ask who knows the word; call on student to say word.

Benchmark Record Keeping
Chart for Literacy Levels

Student's Name _____

Please write date in blank when child demonstrated behavior/strategy.

Benchmarks of Acquisition for the Pre-Emergent Level

Reading

_____ Identifies the front of book.

_____ Knows the difference between print and picture.

_____ Can find a familiar book and pretend read.

_____ Can follow a story as the teacher reads aloud or with a read along tape by turning pages at appropriate time.

_____ Some word and syllable segmentation is evident.

_____ Enjoys selecting books of interest on own to look at and "read" the pictures.

Writing

_____ Attempts some writing (a letter or a word).

_____ Orally tells a story from pictures.

_____ Can reread individual language experience sentence.

Benchmarks of Acquisition for Emergent Level

Reading

_____ Understands how reading goes (left to right).

_____ Understands which part and which page of print is read first.

_____ Can voice print match using the emergent book.

_____ Identifies and explains purpose of period and question mark.

_____ Can identify a capital letter in a sentence.

_____ Understands where the first and last part of a sentence is.

_____ Can word and syllable segment (Use TALS [Sawyer, 1987] to verify).

_____ Orally can summarize book read.

_____ Enjoys being read to and listens attentively.

_____ Using the picture and title on the cover of the book, can predict what story will be about.

_____ Enjoys rereading emergent books.

_____ Developing specific interests in books and selects them on own to read pictures.

Writing

_____ Attempting to convey a message by writing, usually random letters but may have some sound/symbol correspondence.

_____ Draws pictures to convey a message.

_____ Tries to label pictures or writes a message using a few letters or known words like cat, dog, mom, and dad.

Benchmarks of Acquisition for Early 1 Level

Reading

_____ Can identify words from other similar words when the teacher pronounces the words to be identified.

_____ Understands how reading goes when there is more than one line of print (left to right and return).

_____ Orally can state the topic of the book read.

_____ While reading, the student can use initial sounds to pronounce the unknown words.

_____ Enjoys being read to and listens attentively to read aloud.

_____ Can orally summarize read aloud book.

_____ Can identify and explain use of comma, exclamation point, and quotation marks.

_____ Beginning to predict the next part of the story while reading.

_____ Able to recognize words in text by pointing when teacher gives orally.

_____ Able to follow words in text while story is being read and recognizes when words or sentences are out of sequence.

_____ Enjoys rereading Early 1 books independently and/or with a peer.

_____ Can isolate one and two words and letters in print.

_____ Can identify first and last letter of a word in book.

_____ Can read emergent books independently (not first read with teacher) and understands message.

Writing

_____ While writing, the student attempts to use initial sounds to write his/her words.

_____ Can write a sentence using inventive spelling (medial letters or sounds are usually not present).

_____ Attempts to convey a message through writing. Mostly letters are used that correspond somewhat to sounds in words.

Benchmarks of Acquisition for Early 2 Level

Reading

_____ Using an Early 2 book, the child will be able to complete a cloze exercise of 5-7 sentences in length with one blank per sentence. The sentences are directly taken from the text (application of semantic and syntactic cueing strategies).

_____ The child is able to sound segment or distinguish all sounds in a one-syllable word by using markers such as blocks. (Use Sawyer Test [Sawyer, 1987] to verify.)

_____ Demonstrates understanding of story by orally expressing the story events.

_____ Able to read 18 out of 20 familiar sight vocabulary words.

_____ Often selects Emergent, Early 1, or Early 2 books to read on own.

_____ Enjoys being read to and responds to story by relating own experiences to the read aloud story.

Writing

_____ Uses inventive spelling to write a simple story.

_____ Groups of letters are now being used to represent words. Many letters correspond to sounds in words.

_____ Uses similar sentence patterns in writing such as "I like to eat. I like to swim."

Benchmarks of Acquisition for the Early 3 Level

Reading

_____ Can use sound/symbol relationship in dictated sentences presented by the teacher. These sentences are simple and contain words familiar to the child. (Can use Clay [1979] dictation sentences.)

_____ Can complete a cloze exercise consisting of 7 sentences and one blank per sentence. These sentences are taken from the book read.

_____ Can pronounce unfamiliar words in isolation (approximately 20). Some examples are: hint, wave, scrap, sport, and blame. The words follow long, short, and r-controlled vowel rules. This activity assesses one aspect of the graphophonic cueing strategy: the ability to apply sound/symbol relationship for phonetically regular words.

_____ Can respond to book read by orally summarizing story and relating to own experiences.

Writing

_____ Can write a simple story with an awareness of story sequence.

_____ Uses inventive spelling and some conventional spelling to write a simple story.

_____ Attempts to copy an author in writing.

_____ Uses more description in writing to clarify message.

_____ Uses some variety in sentence structure when writing.

Benchmarks of Acquisition for Early 4 Level

Reading

_____ Can orally respond to an Early 4 book by relating own experiences.

_____ Can read an Early 4 book (not read before) and retell the story by writing unassisted.

_____ Can demonstrate application of sound/symbol relationship by reading words following the double vowel rules. These words are not part of the sight vocabulary. Nonsense words may have to be used in this case. Examples: moat, awkward, mention, and outcast.

Writing

_____ Writes a story with evidence of beginning, middle, and end.

_____ Uses inventive spelling and conventional spelling.

_____ Writes using descriptive words to clarify message.

_____ Uses a variety of sentence structures in writing.

_____ Developing an awareness of style in writing.

Benchmarks of Acquisition for Fluency 1 Level

Reading

_____ Can complete a cloze exercise of about 10 sentences with two blanks per sentence taken from the Fluency 1 level text read.

_____ Reads a Fluency 1 book silently and completes story event sequence; that is, the teacher will ask the students to write the main events of the story in sequence.

_____ Can identify major characters and list at least one attribute for each character.

_____ Can orally respond to book relating to own experiences.

Writing

_____ Writing pieces have a beginning, middle, and end with some detail in the development.

_____ Begins to use more complex sentences in writing.

_____ Developing own style of writing.

Benchmarks of Acquisition for Fluency 2 Level

Reading

_____ Able to interpret with support from the book the meaning of the text.

_____ Can complete a written cloze exercise that utilizes words with affixes as word choices.

_____ Can briefly summarize the plot of the Fluency 2 book read silently.

_____ Can write a response to text by relating own experiences and orally using passages from the book to support the response.

_____ Can identify by writing the problem/resolution of a story.

Writing

_____ Writing pieces are cohesive and use descriptive language to clarify message.

_____ Develops at least one area of writing (beginning, middle, or end) using descriptive language, more complex sentences, and images to convey message.

_____ Uses conventional spelling mostly but inventive spelling is still generally used.

Benchmarks of Acquisition for Fluency 3 Level

Reading

_____ Able to complete a literary elements chart with some teacher support. The chart includes:

> Title, author
> Major and minor characters
> Summary of plot

Setting, genre
Problem/resolution
Climax

_____ Can write a response to the Fluency 3 book read silently and give reasons or support for response from the text.

Writing

_____ Writing pieces are cohesive, use descriptive language, and a variety of sentence structures.

_____ Attempting to use other styles or forms.

_____ Writing pieces show some character development.

Benchmarks of Acquisition for Fluency 4 Level

Reading

_____ Can list three statements of fact learned from a nonfiction selection.

_____ Understands a nonfiction selection and can use selection to create a journal entry that integrates the selection and student's experiences.

_____ Can independently complete a literary elements chart.

Writing

_____ Writing pieces are well developed and indicate some use of other styles and forms.

_____ Writing pieces are interesting and present a clear image to the reader.

References

Cambourne, B. (1988). *The Whole Story*. New York: Scholastic.

Clay, M. (1979). *The Early Detection of Reading Difficulties*. Portsmouth, New Hampshire: Heinemann.

Edelsky, C. (1990). Whose Agenda Is This Anyway? A Response to McKenna, Robinson, and Miller. *Educational Researcher*, 19, 7-10.

Graves, D. (1983). *Writing: Teachers & Children At Work*. Portsmouth, New Hampshire: Heinemann.

Griffith, P. and Olson, M. (1992). Phonemic Awareness Helps Beginning Readers Break the Code. *The Reading Teacher*, 45, 516-523.

Holdaway, D. (1979). *The Foundations of Literacy*. New York: Scholastic.

Jones, B. F.; Palincsar, A. S.; Ogle, D. S.; and Carr, E. G. (1987). Learning and Thinking. *Strategic Teaching and Learning: Cognitive Instruction in the Content Areas*. Alexandria, Virginia: Association for Supervision and Curriculum Development (ASCD).

Morrow, L. M. and Rand, M. K. (1991). Promoting Literacy During Play by Designing Early Childhood Classroom Environments. *The Reading Teacher*, 44, 396-402.

Newman, J. M., ed. (1985). *Whole Language Theory in Use*. Portsmouth, New Hampshire: Heinemann.

Reading in Junior Classes. (1985). New York: Richard C. Owens.

Ready to Read Series. (1984). New York: Richard C. Owens.

Rutherford, W.; Hall, G.; and Newlove, B. (1982). *Describing the Concerns Principals Have About Facilitating Change.* Paper presented at the meeting of Amercan Educational Research Assocication, New York, March 1982.

Sawyer, D. J. (1987). *Test of Awareness of Language Segments.* Austin, Texas: Pro-Ed.

Further Resources for Professional Development

Atwell, N. (1987). *In the Middle*. Portsmouth, New Hampshire: Heinemann.

Butler, A. (1988). *The Elements of the Whole Language Program*. Crystal Lake, Illinois: Rigby.

Butler, A. (1988). *Shared Book Experience*. Crystal Lake, Illinois:Rigby.

Butler, A. and Turbill, J. (1984). *Towards a Reading-Writing Classroom*. Portsmouth, New Hampshire: Heinemann.

Calkins, L. M. (1986) .*The Art of Teaching Writing*. Portsmouth, New Hampshire: Heinemann.

Cochrane, O., Cochrane, D., Scalena, S., and Buchanan, E. (1984). *Reading Writing and Caring*. New York: Richard C. Owen.

Getting It Together (1986). Edited by W. McVitty Portsmouth, New Hampshire: Heinemann.

Johnson, T. D. and Louis, D. R. (1987). *Literacy through Literature*. Portsmouth, New Hampshire: Heinemann.

Lynch, P. (1986). *Using Big Books and Predictable Books*. New York: Scholastic.

Mooney, M. E. (1990). *Reading To, With, and By Children*. New York: Richard C. Owen.

Peetoom, A. (1986). *Shared Reading: Safe Risks with Whole Books*. New York: Scholastic.

Routman, R. (1991). *Invitations*. Portsmouth, New Hampshire: Heinemann.

Trelease, J. (1989). *The New Read-Aloud Handbook*. New York: Penguin Books.

Color Code Chart
Defining Literacy Levels for Whole Language

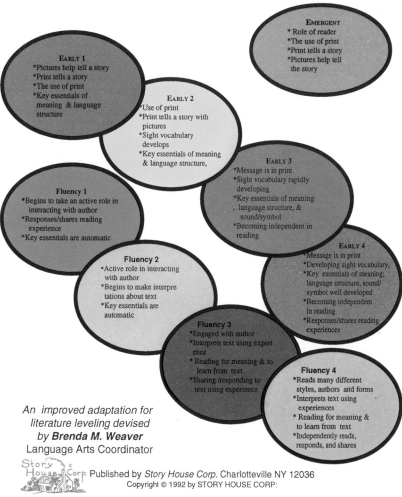

EMERGENT
* Role of reader
* The use of print
* Print tells a story
* Pictures help tell the story

EARLY 1
* Pictures help tell a story
* Print tells a story
* The use of print
* Key essentials of meaning & language structure

EARLY 2
* Use of print
* Print tells a story with pictures
* Sight vocabulary develops
* Key essentials of meaning & language structure,

EARLY 3
* Message is in print
* Sight vocabulary rapidly developing
* Key essentials of meaning, language structure, & sound/symbol
* Becoming independent in reading

EARLY 4
* Message is in print
* Developing sight vocabulary,
* Key essentials of meaning; language structure, sound/symbol well developed
* Becoming independent in reading
* Responses/shares reading experiences

Fluency 1
* Begins to take an active role in interacting with author
* Responses/shares reading experience
* Key essentials are automatic

Fluency 2
* Active role in interacting with author
* Begins to make interpre tations about text
* Key essentials are automatic

Fluency 3
* Engaged with author
* Interprets text using experi ence
* Reading for meaning & to learn from text
* Sharing /responding to text using experience

Fluency 4
* Reads many different styles, authors and forms
* Interprets text using experiences
* Reading for meaning & to learn from text
* Independently reads, responds, and shares

An improved adaptation for literature leveling devised by **Brenda M. Weaver**
Language Arts Coordinator

Published by *Story House Corp.* Charlotteville NY 12036